Through the South with
a Union Soldier

****
Through the South with a

Union Soldier
****

edited by
Arthur H. DeRosier, Jr.

PUBLICATIONS OF
THE EAST TENNESSEE STATE UNIVERSITY
RESEARCH ADVISORY COUNCIL
JOHNSON CITY, TENNESSEE

Alburtus A. Dunham
1836–1863

Charles Laforest Dunham
1842–1929

To

Deborah Ann

Marsha Carol

Charles Arthur

Melissa Estelle

CERTAINLY ONE of the most enduring aspects of American military tradition has been the belief in the superiority of and the necessity for reliance upon the "citizen-soldier." In part, this is grounded in the best democratic tradition for it mirrored the conviction that a free man will fight with more zeal and determination to protect his home and institutions than any "hireling." The thrifty Yankee, likewise, has seen no need for supporting vast numbers of idle men in times of peace. Furthermore, as he understood history, standing armies were always potentially a weapon that might be turned against the very people that they were designed to protect. Steeped in classical and agrarian traditions, the citizen of the United States has always been attracted by the picture of Cincinnatus leaving his plow to hasten to the rescue of his country. Few have doubted that his American counterpart, if he survived his "tour of duty," would return likewise to his plow and reassume his position as backbone of the nation.

Within this assumption, it is easy to visualize an aroused citizenry seizing their arms to hurl back an invading army of foreigners. But what if the enemy were fellow citizens who were not invading but only asking for the democratic right of self determination? For the first time, then, the American Civil War subjected the democratic-army thesis to the test of blood and fire under these abnormal conditions. The verdict in this trial is inscribed upon the pages of the nation's history. But what of the individual, whose character, convictions, and philosophy determined the success or failure of the citizen-soldier concept?

The answer lies in the pages that follow. He could and did think that he was fighting for a cause in which he could believe. As

I have long been convinced, the Civil War was not, to the participant, a fraternal struggle, but rather a war between strangers. It was not by accident that Laforest Dunham, when writing from the South, referred to the North as "America." Although he respected his antagonist, it was a respect based upon fighting ability and not upon any feeling of common brotherhood. True to the picture, the Dunhams came from the soil, longed for it while away, and the survivor did, indeed, return to his plow.

By comparison with similar Civil War materials, this collection of letters has a number of characteristics that set it apart and make it of unusual interest to the lay reader and professional historian alike. In the first place, I can recall no comparable compilation that succeeded so well in leaving me a satisfying sense of "knowing" the author after having read his unstudied words. Written to members of his family, who knew him too well to permit conscious dissimulation, his hasty notes lay bare his personality, hopes, and fears, as well as the mundane facts of his daily existence. This is not an epic depicting on a broad canvas the heroic sweep of battle, but rather a low-keyed account of one man's war: the thoughts and feelings of a citizen-soldier caught up in the necessity of performing what he believes to be his duty.

Equally important is the completeness of the picture that is offered. Thanks to the fact that he wrote often and that apparently most of his letters have survived, we are in the happy position of never losing sight of the author for more than a few weeks at random times, yet even then maintaining the feeling that we know what he is doing. A further advantage is that his messages home cover the entire period of his military service, from enlistment to honorable discharge, thus presenting an evolving story of the conversion of a young farm boy into a battle-hardened man. An added bonus is the fact that his tour of duty and area of service coincides with periods and scenes of combat of unusual interest. Thus, from Louisville, Kentucky, in September, 1862, one can trace the course of a federal army, *via* Atlanta, to Washington, D.C., in May, 1865.

But pre-eminent, in my opinion, is the fact that here we have the personification of "Billy Yank," the average northern citizen-soldier. Here we find the forces that motivated him to enlist and his changing view of the "game" of war. The boredom of inaction is interspersed with the quickened pulse of battle. The callow youth becomes self-reliant, assuring his family, "I will take the best care of myself I can, and I think I am prety good at it." There is pride and *esprit de corps* when he writes, "The same place had ben charged on five times before by our troops and they could not take it, but we took it the first charge." Present also is the studied nonchalance of the seasoned campaigner in his assertion that he had just as soon be on the front line as in the rear and his terse comment that "Good had his right hand shot off by a shell. Once in awhile thare is a ball comes over whare we are but the boys have got so that they dont care mutch about them."

Yet, he has no illusions about war. He does not want his brothers to join the army; of an acquaintance, he wrote, "Soldering is know place for him. One thing he has not got grit enough—he gives up to quick." As far as he himself was concerned, however, his position was clear. "For my part I dont care about going in to annother one [war] but iff they call uppon ous I am ready to do my share." Yet the citizen was never more than momentarily eclipsed by the soldier. In his final letter, he wrote, "I cant leave on account of signing my papers to make a sitizen of myself, and you may bet your life that I ant backward about it."

Certainly one of the most impressive aspects of this collection is the universality of his experiences. No one with military service will fail to identify with Dunham as he characteristically opens each letter with the announcement that he has no "news" to tell but will write nevertheless. How timeless are appeals for more letters from home, the hunger for details of their daily lives, the frank admission of homesickness. Told and retold are the ever present rumors that march with every army, the concern with payday, and the insecurity of not knowing where he is going. Here, likewise, is portrayed the awkward effort to tell of the death of a brother and of friends; of trying to gloss over a term in the guardhouse; and the humor of a trip to the hospital in search of a cure for the "army quick step."

In short, this is a facet in the story of America as told through the life of one of its average citizens. Multiplied by millions, it is our history.

JOHN S. EZELL
David Ross Boyd Professor
of History and Dean of the College of
Arts and Sciences
University of Oklahoma

✳✳✳✳✳✳✳✳✳✳✳✳✳✳✳✳✳✳✳✳✳✳✳✳✳✳✳✳✳✳✳✳✳✳✳✳✳✳*Contents

***Maps

Maps prepared by Mr. Majid Ejlali,
East Tennessee State University Cartographer

*Through the South with
a Union Soldier*

LAFOREST'S TREK FROM HOME TO WAR'S END

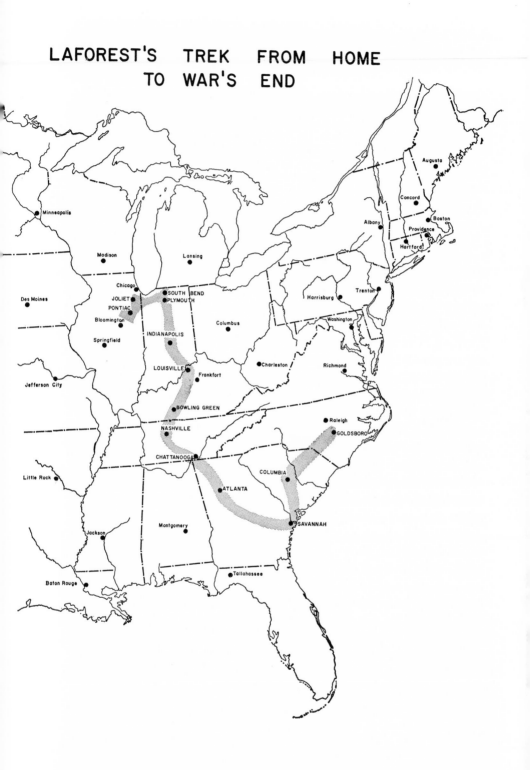

cited about anything, and there were already enough Civil War letters available to keep students of the period busy for decades; I simply thanked Professor Savage, and set the letters aside on my desk. There they might have lain for months, except for my wife's curiosity. When I told Delores about the letters—and how the Dunhams had found them among attic junk in Illinois—she wanted to read and evaluate them. Each day, for a week or so, she asked me about the collection and its obvious worth; every time she mentioned the papers she added the opinion that valuable war secrets were probably contained in the letters and our whole evaluation of the struggle quite possibly would be altered. Finally, she did stir my interest and we read the letters together. As usual, her intuition proved correct; I concluded my reading of the letters convinced that they were not only valuable historic manuscripts, but were also worth publication.

Our knowledge of American history would be richer and fuller if our country were filled with millions of Carroll and Sue Dunhams. How many people have found documents, letters, and bills in the attic or basement and simply disposed of them as dust catchers and fire hazards. When old newspapers are found in the shed, how many people think of saving them and taking them to the nearest library or university. I am afraid that we are collectively guilty of historical negligence, and each year tons of rich national evidence are burned or discarded as junk. Fortunately, there are citizens who are inquisitive and cannot dispose of anything without first assessing its worth: such people are Carroll and Sue Dunham. They just had to know if Alburtus's and Laforest's letters would shed some small bit of light on our understanding of the ordinary Union soldier.

II

Before discussing the contents and importance of the Dunham letters, it seems necessary to tell something of the family and its history. This family was an average American family. They left no indelible mark on American thinking or history; they invented no

I

On a hot July day in 1966, William Savage, Associate Professor of History at Louisiana State University in New Orleans, stopped by my office at the University of Oklahoma to give me a narrow box containing 140 letters written by two Illinois privates during the Civil War. Bill explained to me that the letters belonged to family friends—Mr. and Mrs. Carroll C. Dunham of Oklahoma City. Mr. Dunham, and his wife, Sue, still have an interest in the family farm in Illinois; they periodically return to check on the crops, upkeep of the house and barns, and the general state of affairs. On one recent trip, they explored attics and basements on the property; in an attic they found a collection of old clothes, furniture, and general family junk. Among the family "treasures" they discovered a trunk containing letters written by two ancestors, Alburtus A. and Charles Laforest Dunham, army privates in the Civil War. The trunk contained other Civil War mementos, including uniforms, pictures, and weapons. The letters particularly interested Carroll and Sue Dunham; they removed each from its original envelope, read it carefully, and filed it away chronologically. Convinced that the collection was of historic significance, they took the papers to Bill Savage and told him their convictions. He read the letters carefully but, since he specializes in French history, he could offer the Dunhams no verdict. So he handed me the letters and requested an evaluation for his anxious friends.

I would like to report that I read the letters that very night, and that by the first crack of dawn I knew they were publishable, but such was not the case. It was really too hot that day to get ex-labor-saving tools; they performed no known acts of unusual heroism. They were hard working, pious, strong human beings who did their jobs, lived their lives, and died unnoticed except by kin and friends. This is the prime value of the collection: it is a partial record of an "average" family, whose "average" sons went to war, in an "average" regiment, with an "average" war record. Alburtus and Laforest were simply two men of that mass of average American youth who met their country's call—North and South—and did the best job they could for the cause they represented. It is this view of the average Union private, and his moment on the stage of history, that makes these documents not only interesting but valuable to our understanding of the conflict and the men who shaped it.

Alburtus A. and Charles Laforest—he went by the name of Laforest—were born in Vernon, New York. Their parents—Diantha Maria and Simeon Harlow Dunham—were descendants of New England Puritans from Hartford County, Connecticut. Like many thousands of other New England sons and daughters in search of new land and new opportunities, they married, emigrated to upstate New York and, eventually, to northern Illinois. Simeon was born in 1810, married Diantha in 1835, and immediately moved to New York. Shortly after their arrival in Vernon, Diantha gave birth to her first child, Alburtus, on September 9, 1836; Eugene H. was born on July 28, 1838; Hercey M. on June 23, 1840; Charles Laforest on July 26, 1842; Hiram A. on September 9, 1846; and Casper on March 2, 1853. The latter lived slightly more than one year and died on July 30, 1854. The rest grew to maturity in New York and Illinois, a close knit group that enjoyed the pleasures of working and playing together as a family unit.

Simeon was never satisfied with life in New York. The land was better than that available around Hartford, but still he had arrived late and had taken the second-rate land that was left. When he heard that northern Illinois counties and towns were building on land so black and so rich it defied description, Simeon packed his family and emigrated to Livingston County, Illinois in 1857.

Pontiac, the major town in Livingston County, was surveyed and plotted in 1837. Simeon purchased 160 acres of land in Esmen

Township, approximately six miles northwest of Pontiac, and received his mail at the Rowe Post Office which served Esmen Township. It is obvious that both Alburtus and Laforest loved Illinois, their farm, and their friends, as both often reminisced about their past life and swore never to roam again if the Lord returned them safely to family and friends. They were true sons of the soil. Anything could grow abundantly in the rich soil of agricultural Illinois, on flat, well watered, and rich land. The dark and even black loam of the Pontiac, Fairbury, Bloomington area still commands a visitor's attention. When he hears the natives proudly proclaim that his land is the "buckle" of the corn belt, the visitor can only nod approval. When Laforest scoffed at the agricultural possibilities of the Tennessee hills and mountains, he was comparing their soil with the soil and vegetation of Livingston County, which was not entirely fair. He later came to appreciate Southern agriculture, as his stay in Dixie lengthened and his perspective widened, but he was always the son of a soil known for its fertility and abundance.

Not only did the Dunhams appreciate the richness of soil, but also richness of heritage. Both Simeon and Diantha were practicing Christians and instilled in their sons and daughters an appreciation for the Bible and a fear of God. They went to "meatin" faithfully and read the family Bible together nightly. Since Bible-reading was necessary for salvation, education was necessary for Bible-reading. Much has been written of the Puritans' concern for education in their colony. It was the duty of Puritan parents and society to teach children to read, write, and handle fundamental arithmetic problems: so it was in the Dunham family. Each of the children got all of the education available in Vernon and Pontiac. Note the literacy of Alburtus's letters; one seldom finds a private soldier who handles the language with greater facility. Laforest's grammar, syntax, and spelling are primitive by today's standards, but his writing is quite readable and clear. One reason few collections of letters by Northern and Southern enlisted men exist today is that many privates, especially Confederates, could barely write. Not only did Alburtus and Laforest write with facility, but their penmanship was quite legible. Very few letters are hard to read, except where the ink has run or seeped through the paper, or where pencil-written sentences have faded. Hence, the abundant references to God, church, Bible-reading, and Sunday come through clearly, and we must conclude that their parents had reared the boys well and passed on to them the essential elements of the white American Protestant culture. If we can believe Laforest, as he wrote home from deep within the Confederacy, it was this heritage that sustained his regiment through the costly conflict.

War often descends on people unnoticed and surprises them when it finally arrives. We can look back today on the decade of the 1850's and observe each crisis of the period driving the sections farther and farther apart. It is hard to see how any thinking person could have been surprised when the shouting and bluff ended on April 12 and war became a reality. Most Northerners had heard their Southern brethren threaten secession earlier in the 1830's and 1850's; they thought the threat of secession, after the election of Lincoln, was another bluff to be ignored. Also, a number of compromise efforts were undertaken during Buchanan's last months in office. Many felt, surely, at least one of these efforts would result in a lessening of the tensions between sections. But, of course, nothing worked, and the nation was plunged into bloody civil war which lasted four incredible years.

The Dunhams were Republicans, though not abolitionists, and supported the candidacy of Abraham Lincoln. When he was elected, they wished him well and approved of his early efforts to restore the recalcitrant South to the Union. They, along with other Northern Americans, hoped that Lincoln's call for 75,000 men, plus the blockade and the Regular Army, might crush the rebellion in three months. First Bull Run, and the continued defiance of eleven Southern states, dashed these hopes and brought reality to the Union by the end of 1861.

America settled down to a long and bloody civil war. The President issued a call for 300,000 more volunteers and Livingston County, Illinois prepared to do its part. The 129th Infantry was organized at Pontiac in August of 1862 by Colonel George P.

Smith, and mustered into service on September 8. Five of the companies—A, B, C, E, and G—were filled with young men from Livingston County; four other companies contained men from Scott County and one was formed in Rock Island County. Both Alburtus and Laforest were in Company C, along with many of their friends from Esmen Township. Alburtus was twenty-six and Laforest had just turned twenty. Two other brothers, Eugene, who was twenty-four, and Hiram, soon to be sixteen, remained at home. Very seldom did all eligible brothers in a family enlist at the same time, since some men had to remain to help with farming chores. I cannot explain why Eugene stayed at home while an older and younger brother took up arms. This fact is especially interesting to me since we note in the records that Alburtus was married on September 4 and mustered into the service on September 7, 1862 just three days after his marriage. The letters do indicate that Eugene and Hiram sought to enlist during the conflict, but Laforest and the family at home brought pressure to keep them from enlisting. On September 22, 1862, the 129th Regiment left Pontiac with 927 officers and men, headed toward basic training—and the war.

III

It is always difficult to justify a claim of significance from a purely subjective viewpoint. If significance is defined as something startlingly new or different which alters previous concepts and fosters reinterpretation of a person or event, then I cannot say that the Dunham papers are significant. However, I do not define significance in such narrow bounds. This new collection of letters, by two privates in the Union army, is important and deserves to be studied and evaluated by anyone who would understand the feelings, prejudices, and fears of the common soldier in wartime.

The route of the army is well marked on the maps included in this volume. The 129th Regiment traveled by train from Pontiac, Illinois, to Louisville, Kentucky. After basic training, it joined the Thirty-eighth Brigade of the Twelfth Division of the Army of the

Ohio. On October 3 the men marched south from Louisville to keep General Braxton Bragg and his army from threatening the city. They followed Bragg to Frankfort, Danville, and Crab Orchard, Kentucky, without making contact. On October 17, the Thirty-eighth Brigade was transferred to the Tenth Division, with Brigadier General R. S. Granger commanding. The army again took up the chase on October 20 and headed toward Bowling Green, Kentucky, by way of Danville, Perryville, and Munfordville. On November 21 the 129th was sent as a garrison to protect the railroad at Mitchellville, Tennessee.

From the middle of November, 1862, until early June, 1863, the 129th guarded the railroad from Bowling Green to Gallatin, Tennessee. Frequent clashes with rebels in the mountainous terrain of north-central Tennessee are recorded in the letters. Though no pitched battles were fought, Laforest got his first taste of combat in Tennessee, chasing rebel guerrillas through the mountains and protecting the railroad from saboteurs. Alburtus, sick and weak almost since the beginning of his enlistment, succumbed to "brain fever" on January 17, 1863, and died in Fountain Head, Tennessee.

In early June, 1863, the 129th Regiment was transferred to Gallatin, Tennessee, to be garrisoned at Fort Thomas. The men defended the fort against threatened attacks by General John H. Morgan who brought his army to within eight miles of the fort, but retreated without challenging the Union defenses to pitched battle.

On August 22, 1863, the regiment was sent to Nashville and remained there until the end of February, 1864. By this time, the 129th was reassigned to the First Brigade of the Third Division of the Twentieth Corps. Laforest and his friends defended Nashville, watched the rivers in the vicinity, and continued to protect the railroads from Confederate harassment. Throughout his long stay in central Tennessee, Laforest observed much of the state and had much of interest to say about its people and their plight during wartime.

By late February, 1864, the 129th moved south to Murfreesboro, Chattanooga, Lookout Mountain, and then into Georgia with General William T. Sherman. On the march toward Atlanta, they fought in the battles of Resaca, Buzzard's Roost, Lost Mountain, Dallas, Peach Tree Creek, and Atlanta itself. From Atlanta, they pushed on with Sherman toward Savannah in November, 1864. No letters were written or preserved during this period. The 129th halted near Savannah on December 10th, and, after a short rest, traveled into the Carolinas. They reached Columbia, the capital of South Carolina, and turned north toward Fayetteville, Bentonville, and Goldsboro, North Carolina. The 129th played a significant role in an important encounter with the enemy at Bentonville, their last battle of the war. Peace, thankfully, came in April, 1865, and the 129th participated in the national review of troops in Washington, D.C. The regiment mustered out of the service on June 8, 1865, and traveled by rail from Washington to Chicago. As Laforest rode the few remaining miles from Chicago to Pontiac—and thought back over the past two years and nine months of service—he sadly lamented: "Just think what a change thare is since I left home."

This short summary of the route of the 129th has little to do with an evaluation of the Dunham letters. We know the exact route of all United States and Confederate armies; we also know the commanders, strategy, successes, and failures of each. We have biographies of almost all of the commanders and countless monographs relating what each brigade and regiment was doing most of the time. But there is a void in our knowledge of many aspects of Civil War campaigning. What do we know about the life and lot of the private soldier? We know where he was and how successful he was in battle, but that is not enough for understanding. Precious little information is available on the more important subjects of what he thought, what he feared, what he ate, and whom he hated.

Lack of important information clouds our understanding of the private soldier in the Civil War. We have few collections of soldiers' letters compared to those of officers and politicians. The enlisted man was constantly on the move, with eighty or more pounds of equipment to strap on his back and waist, he could hardly burden himself with such nonessentials as letters. Conversely, the friends and family of enlisted men were not likely to see the need for keeping the letters for posterity and future historians. Many were thrown away soon after receipt; more were disposed of in various ways during the intervening years; and only relatively few collections numbering over twenty letters have survived to this day.

A second factor has hindered our understanding of the private just as severely as has the lack of research material: we have misused what we have at our disposal. Many historians, unfortunately, have tried to make a hero, buffoon, philosopher, or rogue out of the common soldier by extracting a sentence or two from a letter or a collection of letters and arranging them to prove a preconceived thesis. Why not study all of the soldier's letter—or, better still, why not look at an entire collection and see what the historian has at his disposal? Why extract the flashy or vulgar sentence to prove that the Civil War soldier was tough, soft-hearted, homesick, or anything else? Why not approach him as an ordinary person, a mixture of good and bad, wise and unwise, prophetic and short-sighted, scared and brave.

The value of this manuscript collection is that it fits the needs expressed above, it is a rather large collection of letters that shows the many sides of a young man at war. A few of the themes that one observes in the collection will be mentioned here. It should be remembered, though, that these comments mention only a few of the subjects upon which the Dunhams expressed opinions. They are mentioned simply to introduce students to the letters, and not as a complete listing of major subjects discussed. Some of the comments concern important subjects, such as the Union soldiers' opinion of the Negro; others relate the feelings Laforest had when he met, talked, and ate with Confederate civilians.

Many of the letters offer information on minor matters of concern to the average soldier, not historically important. They are all voiced by the same person, and mirror his concern on subjects about which he felt strongly enough to write home to folks and express an opinion. It is defensible to claim that Laforest spoke for most of his comrades when he offered an opinion; possibly he more nearly mirrors the sentiments of fellow privates in the Union forces than do the ranking officers in their letters home to wife or mother. A review of the Dunham correspondence will not only inform us of the private soldier's fears when he entered battle, but will also tell us much more about other subjects we must study to know him as a human being. It was his war; he did the fighting and you cannot applaud or hiss merely on the evidence of excerpts and selected sentences.

Alburtus was six years older than Laforest. At twenty-six, he was mature, settled, and saw the war as a job that must be completed. From the beginning, Alburtus was the letterwriter of the two. He wrote the long newsy letters about boot-training and the Kentucky years. Now and then Laforest would add a short P.S. to one of Alburtus's letters, or forward brief ones of his own, but they contained little information and less news. Alburtus was a precise correspondent who wrote long involved letters which described in detail the movements of the army and the conflict he observed. He seldom strayed from the subject, and he offered his reader little breadth and a great deal of detail. We learn his precise weight, the exact mileage between towns or points, and accurate and involved weather reports. His letters are easy to follow, but are lifeless and often very impersonal. For example, if one did not know that Sarah Jane Nigh Dunham was Alburtus's bride of three short days before the regiment was ordered to Louisville, you would think she was a sister or a casual friend. There is none of the information that husband and wife or lovers share with each other, just the same prosaic details that Alburtus wrote to Hiram and his parents. It is hard to develop a rapport with this man from reading the letters. He was quiet, thoughtful, and somewhat of a loner. However, we are indebted to him for much information, even though it is knowledge that is generally available elsewhere. The reader is saddened by his early death after only four months in the service and no contact with the enemy. Alburtus never adjusted to the out-of-doors life of the common soldier, and succumbed to colds, congestion, and what Laforest called "brain fever."

When I first read the letters, the death of Alburtus left me feeling sad, and perhaps discouraged. I did not look forward to Laforest's letters for he had contributed little to the previous correspondence. He appeared to be scatterbrained and immature. He developed no subjects, offered off-the-cuff remarks about myriad topics, and seemed to be enjoying himself. During the early days of army life, he was excited about the glamor and newness of war. Farming had become a bit of a drag, and he was ready to see the exciting outside world away from Esmen Township. The war had thus far been bungled by the Union, he reasoned, and the 129th would simply have to roll up its collective sleeves and whip the enemy in a heated battle or two. On November 27, 1862, he cockily wrote to his mother, "It is the opinion of mose evry one that we will be back by spring." He often included this contemporary salutation in his early letters: "All well and right side up." And indeed it was right side up for Laforest who was having a good time observing Kentucky and not meeting the enemy on the field of battle.

Yet, surprising as it might seem, it was Laforest who made the Dunham letters valuable. His apparent literary weaknesses turned out to be his strengths. His letters are less detailed than Alburtus's, but they contain discussions of every subject that caught his fancy. He does not dwell on the movement of armies or present other military information available elsewhere, but spends time discussing politics, philosophy, substitutes, copperheads, and Negroes. We learn how a soldier made hard tack digestible; how he built a shelter or pitched a tent and distributed household chores; we are treated to an observation on the lot of the Army mule and what it smells like to march between hundreds of dead mules that line the highways carrying the army south. It is the discussion of everyday life, with its boredom, humor, pathos, and rewards, that makes these letters a truly significant find. They tell us of the aspirations of the common foot soldier in his own language and style.

We notice manuscript references to subjects of current interest to most Civil War military historians. For example, Laforest had nothing but harsh words for the Negro and his plight. For the most part, Laforest displayed Christian charity and restraint when dealing with others, with problem drinkers or syphilitics, but he always damned Negroes. In one letter Laforest complained: "A cursed nigger is thought more of than a soldier in this war. I tell you what is the fact, I have seen a black devil a rideing in an ambulance that could walk just as well as not and a poor soldier come along that could hardly drag one foot after the other and wanta ride but know you cant ride you ar just glaging off." On another occasion, he registered utter disgust with an old acquaintance back home who contemplated accepting a commission in a Negro regiment. His harsh comments about Negroes are not really out of character for the Northern soldier, and offer us an insight into an aspect of army social life and history that has received considerable attention from historians. These and other letters make it obvious that the Union soldier had no more respect for Negroes and their potential than did soldiers south of the Mason-Dixon line. The Southern soldier believed in white supremacy, but he also took seriously the need for the ruling whites to look after less fortunate blacks. The Northern soldier was fighting, not for black dignity and freedom, but for the Union and Lincoln's belief that it must remain intact to survive.

Another theme that permeates the letters is the respect of the Union soldier for the Confederates' fighting ability, intermingled with the belief that the war could not possibly last more than a few months. It was always going to end after the next conclusive battle. Indeed, from Laforest's letters one can see why this belief was consistently maintained. He mentions the constant stream of Confederate deserters and prisoners, bedraggled, starving, and without proper equipment. The enemy always displayed a fierce determination to win or die trying, and Laforest respected him for his courage. The Confederates were almost without mules and horses, Laforest wrote, and it was impossible for them to last much longer. But they did remain a formidable foe, and his respect for the enemy increased along with his anguish and homesickness. After years of believing the end of the conflict would come with the one major battle, Laforest learned caution and informed his parents on July 16, 1864: "I think iff Grant is successful thare at Ritchmond

the show will wind up this winter, but iff he is not three more years
wont any more than see the end of it."

Besides his remarks on the length of the conflict and Confederate ability to persevere against overwhelming odds are numerous
comments about "traitors" back home. Laforest and his colleagues
had no use for copperheads, substitutes, and George McClellan.
Conversely, they offered effusive praise for Abraham Lincoln and
his conduct of the war. All of these comments are in the letters and
offer a plausible reason, from the Union soldier's vantage point,
why the Confederates were not succumbing to inevitable defeat. A
few random selections from various letters show the soldier's in-
tense feeling. Concerning copperheads, Laforest wrote: "The war
would have ben ended before now if them cowardly whelps at the
north had of kept thare mouths shut and not have doen anything
else. Ile bet that they will get paid back in thare own coin when the
soldiers get back to America again." On another occasion he said:
"I tell you what it does me to heare that some of them copperheads
were drafted. I think it will learn some of them a lesson. If it hadent
ben for them the war would have ben ended now." On the subject
of substitutes in the North, Laforest was just as outspoken:
"Hercy said in her letter E.[ugene] & H.[iram] said if they could
get 2000$ that they would go as a substitute. If I was thare they
could not pille up mony enough in a weak to get me to go for one
of the cowardly whelps." The election of 1864 and the chances of
McClellan and Lincoln at the polls, brought forth these comments:
"We ar a going to have an election in our Regiment today just to
see how the Regiment would go if we was whare we could vote. I
know if I was whare I could vote I would give old Abe a lift. I
would just as soon vote for Jeff Davis at once as to vote for
McClen runing on the platform that he is, but I think thare is know
doubt but what old Abe will get elected. I know he would if the
soldiers all had a chance to vote." After the regimental election,
Laforest stated: "We had an election in the Regiment today and
Father Abe got 286, and Mack got thirty, so you can see how the
soldiers would go if they had a chance. Old Abe is the man to run
this show."

These are only a few of the many subjects discussed in the Dunham letters. They not only treat us to a soldier's-eye view of the struggle, but also allow us to observe the evolution of a young man into a mature adult. The confident and jovial Laforest of September, 1862, became a thoughtful, observant person as the war continued. We see what God came to mean to a person who constantly walked with death; and we observe the predicaments that can befall a young man who is exposed to tobacco, whiskey, and fast women. As most other young men do, Laforest lived through it all and emerged a person whose main goal was to survive the slaughter, return to his farm and plow, and settle down to the peaceful and uncomplicated life of a small farmer.

I would like to commend to the reader Laforest's remarks on the countryside through which he traveled. As an observant farm boy, he offered innumerable comments on soil conditions, fences, mules, orchards, and crops. At times, he underestimated the fertility of Southern soil, and shook his head in wonder at the Tennessee and Georgia mountains and their lack of fertility. Observing the farm area around Richland, Tennessee, in April, 1863, Laforest offered this comment: "Thare is a going to be a great deal of fruit heare this season peach treas are loded down. That is all this country is fit for just to rais fruit know wonder that this state rebeld." However, for the most part, his comments on the South, particularly Tennessee, are thoughtful and offer us an unusual view of the region. He tells us what crops might grow in different soils and pays close attention to the price of agricultural goods in the nearby communities. He is not at all impressed with the cities of Tennessee, especially Nashville, for he saw those places after they were considerably disrupted by cannon fire and, sometimes, fierce fighting.

Laforest Dunham was a young man with a broad perspective. He observed and related his observations to family and friends who were more anxious about his safety than his historical accuracy. His story did have a happy ending for he married Katie Gurnsey, a sweetheart back home, and moved to Avoca, Iowa, where they farmed a small plot of ground until his death in 1929, after a long

and useful life in the occupation of his choosing. However, even
more important for posterity, his old Civil War letters were kept,
replaced in their old envelopes, and stored for future discovery.
Possibly they were put away by Mrs. Dunham before her death on
January 12, 1866; more likely they were placed there by Annis W.
Curtiss Dunham, Simeon's second wife whom he married on October 4, 1869.

IV

It seems a long time since Bill Savage entered my office and
deposited these letters on my desk. The original letters have since
been returned to Mr. and Mrs. Dunham in Oklahoma City. However, a flow copy of all the letters has been deposited in the
Manuscripts Division, Bizzell Library, at the University of Oklahoma. They are cataloged and are now available for general use.

Naturally, the letters themselves were the main research
source I had to use. However, much additional research had to be
completed to identify the numerous soldiers, places, events, and
friends back home who were introduced into the correspondence.
This laborious task could not have been completed successfully if it
had not been for the files made available to me by the Livingston
County Service Officer of the Illinois Veterans' Commission. This
gentleman, Marshall G. Follett, could not have been more generous
with his material, time, and knowledge of the area. Also, the family
records and history supplied by Carroll and Sue Dunham were an
indispensable aid in identifying off-springs and neighbors mentioned in the letters.

I should mention a few especially useful printed sources before I close this introductory chapter. *The History of Livingston
County, Illinois Containing A History of the County—its Cities,
Towns, etc.* . . . (Chicago: William LeBaron, Jr., & Co., 1878)
was a valuable reference to correct spelling of names and points of
local history. Volume VI of the *Report of the Adjutant General of
the State of Illinois* (Springfield: Journal Company, Printers &
Binders, 1900) was the best source available on the composition of

the companies in the 129th Illinois Regiment. Last, William F. Amann (ed.), *Personnel of the Civil War* (New York: Thomas Yoseloff, 1961), was helpful in supplying regimental information and overall command assignments.

Many secondary sources were consulted, but two deserve special mention. Stanley F. Horn, *The Army of Tennessee, A Military History* (Indianapolis: The Bobbs-Merrill Co., 1941); and Alma Lewis-James, *Stuffed Clubs and Antimacassars, Accounts and Tales of Early Fairbury, Illinois* (Fairbury: Record Printing Company, 1967) presented some valuable local color and early history which helped me understand the area around Pontiac and the early culture of Livingston County.

It is my sincere hope that the reader will find the following Dunham letters as informative and enjoyable as I have found them. I have tried to disturb the original letters as little as possible. Both Alburtus and Laforest had a penchant against paragraphing and using punctuation in proper places; therefore, some of both had to be supplied for clarification and understanding. Also, a number of footnotes were added to the text and follow the appropriate letters. More footnotes, commas, spelling corrections, and general editing could have been added with, I believe, disastrous results. It is my earnest opinion that these letters belong to Alburtus and Laforest and not to the editor. The text should remain as pure as possible, with footnotes and corrections offered sparingly and only when absolutely necessary to shed light on the contents or persons under discussion. If this has been done reasonably well, and the editor has remained in the background, then he has fulfilled his role and presented an interesting and valuable collection of Civil War papers for your consideration.

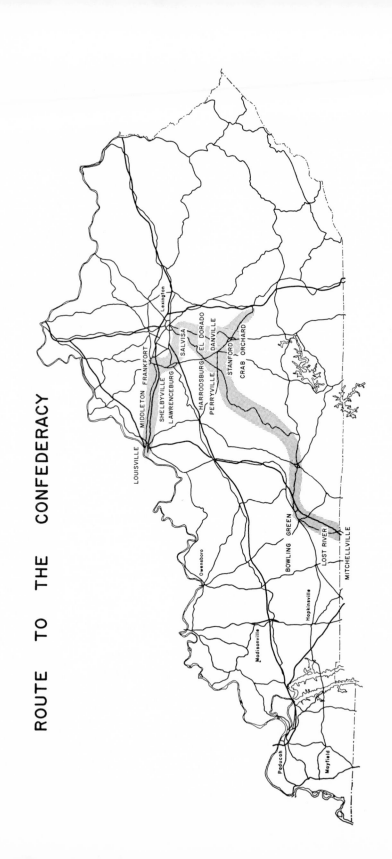

ROUTE TO THE CONFEDERACY

The Kentucky Letters
September 29–November 18, 1862

To Mr. and Mrs. Simeon Harlow Dunham, Sister, and Brother

Louisville, Kentucky, September 29 and 30, 1862

I suppose you are anxious to hear how we are getting along. We are still at Louisville but do not know how long we shall stay here maybe a month and we may leave in 24 hours. Louisville is quite a pleasant place. It is situated on the bank of the Ohio, it is quite a large place. We are about two miles south of town on picket guard. We came out here yesterday morning and expect to go back today. Night before last the pickets took 15 prisoners, the cavelry shot two as dead as mud. They told them to halt and they would not do it. There was good deal of cannonading in the east last night but do not know what it was for. When we arrived here all (*We have just arrived at our camp in town, I am at a house*) Manufacturing and a great many of the stores were closed for it was rumered the night before that Bragg[1] and his whole force was within three miles of the City and all that could [be] packed up [was] and went across the river to Jeffersonville, and ale of the government wagons. But they sone come back since Buell,[2] and his whole force is here now about 150,000 strong. There is about 250,000 soldiers here now. The city is covered with tents, soldiers, & wagons and on the outskirts for several miles. We took one secesh prisoner last night brought him to town with us. He said he was from Bragg's army. He is in the lockup. Some think he is a spy but he said he ran away from Bragg's army. . . . The City is a general uproar or was last night, it is getting a little quieter now. Cannon was heard in the East and it was rumored that Bragg & some of the generals was comeing upon us and all of the soldiers in the city got into battle aray. We have to get into line of battle

1. General Braxton Bragg, Confederate commander of forces between Virginia and the Mississippi River. Bragg and his forces were scaring Americans in the Midwest. He sent Kirby Smith as far north as Covington, Kentucky, but never crossed the Ohio River.
2. General Don Carlos Buell, commander of the Army of the Ohio.

every morning at 9 o clock. There was some skirmishing at a place called Madisonville (so report says.)

I will give a short history of our journey here. After leaving Pa went to Joliet[3] and took supper on crackers and cheese, then took the cut off to M. City at breakfast thence to Indian apolis took supper (slept in the cars two nights) arriving at Jeffersonville the next morning about 8 o clock. Stayed there until after dinner thence to Louisville. Tell E. & H.[4] to take care of themselves for I cannot be with them. We are all well. A. Ross[5] has been quite sick but is in camp today. *Tell E. that I say that if he knows when he is well off to never join the ARMY if he wants to know why tell him I say so. I have good reasons for saying so and Hiram to.* and to stay at home and be a *good boy*. I must close for it is getting late and I want to write to *Jane*[6] this afternoon, and forest[7] wants to say a few words to all. As ever I remain Afft. Son & Brother A. A. Dunham.

Sept. 30 (did not finish yesterday). P.S. I concluded to take another half sheet so I thought I would fill this out. The report is that Buell is superseded by Genl. Thomas,[8] his men seam to all be glad of it. They say that if B.[uell] had been a mind to he could have taken Br.[agg] and his whole force at Green River, but Buell stopped them and let Bragg pass out (Buell is brother-in-law to Bragg). It is said that Thomas is a good genl. We intend to go up

3. Alburtus and his younger brother Laforest traveled with their father from their hometown of Pontiac to Joliet, Illinois. There they left Mr. Dunham, boarded a train that took them east to Michigan City, Indiana, and then south to Indianapolis and Jeffersonville in southern Indiana on the Ohio River. Later, they crossed the river and began basic training at Louisville, Kentucky.

4. Eugene and Hiram Dunham were brothers who remained home in Livingston County.

5. Aaron Ross was a close friend from Livingston County who enlisted on August 6, 1862, rose to the rank of sergeant, and was discharged with the rest of Company C on June 8, 1865.

6. Jane was Alburtus's wife.

7. Forest is the family nickname for Laforest.

8. The report Alburtus refers to was incorrect. At this time General George Henry Thomas was a major-general of volunteers in General Buell's army. Later, Thomas refused to supercede Buell and served well under General Rosecrans.

town today and get our pictures taken. One of the cavelry boys was [shot] yesterday when he went to water his horse at the river. There is secesh a mungst us. But they are good union whilst we are here. There is a good many as handsome places as I ever saw vacated and running to reck. Most every night when we are on dress parade. The Southern gentry ride out in nice curages with a nigger driver to show themselves. There is good many Negroes here. Some are slaves. Good by. Write often and all the news. Your Afft. Son & Brother, A. A. Dunham.

To Hiram Dunham

Louisville, Kentucky, September 30, 1862

I thought you would like to hear from me as Bert [9] is a writing to all so I thought I would drop you a few lines. First plase I have just ben to breakfast and I am so full I can hardly write. The drum is beating for drill but I am a going to give them the slip. We was out on a picket duty on Sunday. We had a fine time. We had all the pancakes we could eat. Our company was held as a reserve through the day and then they put on duble picket at night, so we had a fine time a laying in the shade. Joseph Bar and Bill Brown and others that went in Mil[l]ers Batery [10] just arrived heare last nite. I gues they will go with us. The corn crop heare looks very well whare thare is any, but a general thing it looks like distruction the corn picked and the fences all down, what is not burnt up. Potatoes are 75 cts a bushel, buter 30 cts a pound, whisky the same and cant get it at that. Tel J. W. [11] that we inquired about his brother at indionapolis and that [his] company had left 3 hours before us for heare, and we have not had time to hunt him up. You

9. Bert is the family nickname for brother Alburtus.

10. Though a number of soldiers from Livingston County were named Barr and Brown, no record was found of either of the young men mentioned. This does not mean that Laforest incorrectly identified the two men; it simply means that I have uncovered so many soldiers named Barr and Brown that I cannot pinpoint the exact persons mentioned.

11. A friend at home, Joseph Wilson.

all write son. Write all the news you can think of and how you are getting along with your work. Your affect. Bro. Laforest.

TO MRS. SIMEON H. DUNHAM AND SISTER HERCEY

Louisville, Kentucky, October 2, 1862

As Sheriff Maples [12] started for Pontiac last eve he told me he would fetch another needle case for me when he came back, which I expect will be in a weak of Sundays. I lost my needle case and all that went in it the day we landed in Jeffersonville. Put it in my shirt pocket. I felt in the pocket to see if thare was any hole in it. The bottom was tight and I thought it would be safe, but come to look again I found the side all open from top to bottom. If you could make me another and send it to me it would be quite acceptable. Last evening as we came in from supper the Michigan 33rd laying within six rods of us had a man shot. Thare was two of them fooling with a gun and it went of and shot one of them so that he died in a few minutes. Buell's army left here yesterday to surround Bragg. We are left in reserve with 60 or 70 other Brigades to meet him if Buell shoud succeed in driving him this way. Telegraph report came here yesterday morning that Jeff Davis had asked Old Abe to settle and good many friends thinks he will do it; if so we will be home in two months. [13] We are a going to try to get our pictur taken today. Good bye, As ever I remain your Afft son and brother A. A. Dunham.

P.S. I forgot to say to Pa that he can let what money there is comeing to me out for more than I have to pay the county (so that

12. Edward R. Maples was sheriff of Livingston County from 1860 through 1862.

13. Throughout the papers Alburtus and Laforest continually mention the fact that the Confederates cannot hold out any longer and that they will surely surrender and come to the conference table in the near future. It was more than wishful thinking as most Union soldiers expected the rebels to crack and sue for peace at any moment. Note also the numerous rumors of a halt in the fighting that seemed eminent in order to give the South an opportunity to negotiate without losing face.

I can get it most any time.) for if I live to get back I mean to fetch a stand of mules with me. Thare is some of the best mules heare I ever saw. They are high now but as quick as this war is over they will be cheap. He can do as he thinks is best. A. A. Dunham.

To the Family

Camp near Louisville, Kentucky, October 7, 1862

All well and right side up. Report is here that our troops have taken Lexington. We are within 40 miles of L'on. The rebels were here last week but left when they heard we were comeing. We were on picket night before last and on march in morning. Good bye, healthy here not a sick man in our company. A. A. Dunham.

To Mr. & Mrs. Simeon H. Dunham

Near Louisville, Kentucky, October 7, 1862

I now take the opportunity to drop you a few lines to let you know that we arrived safe and sound. We are about a mile and a half from the Ohio river. There is about 75,000 soldiers in Louisville and here. The talk is that we will go to Louisville this afternoon. The rebbels were advancing on Louisvill yester day but thay are now re treating. I can't write any more for the mail is agoing to start son. I will write the particulars the next time. You had better wait til you hear from us before you write. Your afft. son, C. L. Dunham.

To Mr. Eugene Dunham

Crab Orchard, Kentucky, October 17, 1862

I expect you have been looking for a letter from us before this, but we have been on the go ever since the 3d. so I have not had an opportunity. And another thing we have [written] two letters home, and I have written two to Jane and have not received an answer from any of them. Delos Robinson has received several, also Dave Finley, Lige Schlouser.[14] I heard that the water was very high so I did not think so strange in not receiving a letter from Jane, and others living on Scuttering Creek,[15] have not received any of Gregory [16] & others. Are all well? I was rather under the weather for a day or two but am comeing out all right. Forest is all right. We left Louisville the 3d and have been on the go ever since until last evening when we stopped here but do not know how long we will stay here. We may lieve here in 24 hours and we may stay as many days. Military life is very uncertain. They have poped us through ever since we left L. at a 2.40 gate. If a person wants to try and see what they can endure let them try soldering, for it will kill or cure. The greatest trouble we have is water. It has not rained much here since last spring and is very dusty. If you had have seen us some days you could not have thought it was the 129th. We are camped on the bank of a creek. (it is good water) about 30 . . .[17] m. South of Sanford,[18] Lincoln Co. Ky. It the roughest Country I ever was in. It is all hills and rocks from Louisville to Sanford, great many beautiful places are deserted and their owners are in the *secesh army*. Some of the towns look desolate and are running to rack. I will now give you a discription of our travels since we left Louisville. We left there the 3d of Oct about 4 o clock in the afternoon; marched until 2 o clock at night Oct. 4; rebel spy taken and shot at Shelbyville; passed through South Boston, Shelbyville 36 m from L.[ouisville]. Camped in a cornfield. Oct. 5 man shot in leg and had a good deal of fuz for disturbing a house, the place where I

14. Delos Robinson, David Finley, and Elijah Sclosher were all members of Company C and friends from back home in Livingston County. Robinson rose to the rank of sergeant and Sclosher to corporal by the end of the conflict. All three made it through the conflict alive and were discharged with Laforest on June 8, 1865.

15. Scuttering Creek is really Scattering Point Creek which runs through Amity Township in Livingston County.

16. Thomas J. Gregory was a Livingston County boy in Company C. He enlisted on August 14, 1862 and was discharged on March 10 of the following year.

17. Part of the handwriting is unintelligible in this part of the letter.

18. The town referred to here is Stanford, Kentucky.

got that Book. P. Guard, Oct 6, 2½ m from Camp. P. Guard, washed today, man wounded (there is a great many wounded, and one man killed since we lefe L. By being careless with pistols one of the Scott Co. men shot another whilst looking at his pistol so that he died in five minutes.) A man wounded in foot. Changed Camp half mile west. 8th Marched, passed through Shelbyville, Middletown, camped 11 O clock at night after a march of 20 miles slept till 2 o clock, started for Frankfort, 16 miles distant got there at daylight. 9, Battle of Bardstown. Our advance guard of cavelry had a skirmish with secesh cavelry whiped them, had 3 killed, they 15 killed and wounded, camped in edge of town. At 5 o clock changed camp to a bluff west of Town ¾ of a mile above the level of the city to support a Battery. (F[rankfort] is the poorest and smallest place for the capital of a state I ever saw. I had rather live in P.[ontiac] than to live there by all odds.) 10th. 2 rainy this morning, rainy most of the day. 11th. Started on a force march after the rebbels went to Rough & Ready, 8 m. from F. took dinner, there to Lawrenceburg, 8 miles from Ruff & Ready, camped until 3 o clock next morning. Took one prisoner. Sun. 12th. Started on a force march after rebels, captured 4 and came back again, saw two horses killed day before in a fight. A tramp of 14 miles. Our cavelry took 54 secesh Cavelry and one Major, rainy. Mon. 13. Camped at Salvisa, Mercer Co. 10 m. from Lawrenceburg. Scott Co. man shot by another by a pistol. Tues. 14. El Dorado 6 m. from S. Herrodsburg [*sic*] [Harrodsburg] 12,000 prisoners taken in the fight at Perryville (they are all poorly clad and drassed in Ky. (khaki) janez. I have not seen one with a uniform on, most of them say that if they get back they will stay there.) Danville, camped after a march of 18 m. W. of Sanford, Lincoln Co. Camped until 3 o clock next morning (very rough and rocky country) 15 m. from Danville. Thurs. 16. Crab-Orchard, battle here yesterday, 6 secesh on the field not buried. D. Howard [19] went and saw them. He said they had ben so tramped by cavelry that their faces were all cut up. Camped 6 m from C. Orchard on the Bank of a creek, good water.

19. David Howard, a private in Company C, enlisted on August 9, 1862 and died on November 17, 1864.

Sat. 18. Still at camp under marching orders, expect to lieve camp now. Do not know where we will go. Tell Pa that I wish he would send us some *postage stamps* for we cannot get them here. (We have to write on our letters, soldiers letter) and let you pay for them. We have not had any mail for several days, hope we will get some soon. When you write give us all the particulars for we do not know how things are going on there. We heard last night that Richmond was taken and burnt. Bragg, is headed to Cumb.[erland] Gapp. Do not know but we will have to follow *him*. We mett McCook's division the other day.[20] Our train and his I gess would reach 10 miles. There is part of Woods, Rusaros, and Grangers divisions here amounting to about 125,000 men.[21] Our division is under Granger. 38 Brigade, 10th Division of the Army of the Ohio. Give our love to all. Tell Gault & Robert & the rest of the Boys to take care of themselves for I can't always be with them. Tell Hercey and the rest to write often, and to go over and see Jane as often as she can and not wate for us for if they keep us going as they have done we will not have much time. We will write every opportunity. We have not received any pay yet. If we are stationed we expect to receive it next month. Then we will send some home. Tell Pa to take care of my things best. L. is writing a letter to John Gurney.[22] All of the boys from your section of the country are well. When you can write tell how the folks are getting all the war news. You have plenty of time Sundays. We know no Sunday here; we march Sundays as well as any other day. We had prayer meeting here last evening. I would like to have you a few minutes some evening to see the different things that are going on. Some swearing at the praying and singing. Others makeing a mock of it, some writeing letters, others talking about takeing Bragg and his army, and every thing else you can think of good or bad all talking at once, just think of over a thousand men talking at once. Tell Wil-

20. Reference is made here to General Edwin M. McCook.
21. Alburtus is referring to Generals Thomas J. Wood, Lovell H. Rousseau, and R. S. Granger. The latter was a brigadier-general and commanded the Illinois 129th.
22. John Guernsey, a friend back home in Esmen Township.

son & Tom to write and not wate for us for we will write them as
soon as we have time. Good bye for I must close. Take care of
yourself & old woman. Gather good lots of nuts for us for we expect to be home next spring to eat some of them. If you stay in
Livingston this winter take your team and take Hercey & Janes
land (any others of course), but I now in particular. How is L.
Nigh,[23] and some others getting along, you know who I mean. As
ever I remain your afft. brother A. A. Dunham. P. S. We went to
prayer meeting last evening. Preaching today by Mr. Scott from
Scott Co. a Baptist preacher, have never heard him but they say he
is a very smart man. We are going. Tell Hercey to be a good gail or
I will spank her without a P. over it. A. A. Dunham.
Sunday 19th. Did not have time to finish this until today. P.S. Are
still in camp. Report here that the order from Lincoln is to stop
fighting for 90 days to make a settlement. Do not know how true it
is? Hope it is so. P.S. I forgot to say in the other sheet that Mr.
Hoyle [24] told me to send his best respects to my wife mother and
sister and that he would be happy to see them.
P.S., I gues they will remember him, he was the man that they
liked so well that passed us out at the gate in Pontiac several times.
He is a first trate man the boys ale like him. Capt. Perry [25] is very
sick most of the time. I must close it is so dark that I cannot see.
Dont let any of the girls get you down. A. A. Dunham. Maples
came here last night about 12 o clock and brought that case (I am
thousand times oblige to you) I got a letter from Jane, and your
letters. It makes me feel good to hear from some of you. Will
answer as soon as possible. Mother Nigh sent me some snuff in
Janes letter. We are stand[ing] in a line with our napsacks on our
backs ready for a march (do not know where we are going). I am

23. In this letter reference is made to L. Nigh and Mother Nigh; the former
is Jane Dunham's sister, Lydia, and the latter her mother.
    24. This name is badly spelled; it really refers to 2nd Lt. Stephen H. Kyle
from Nevada Township. Lt. Kyle enlisted on September 8, 1862 and died on
December 1 of the same year.
    25. Captain John B. Perry of Rook's Creek Township was the commanding
officer of Company C. He enlisted on September 8, 1862 and was honorably
discharged on November 21, 1864.

writing on a plate. L. is holding it. Good bye I must close for they will close the mail soon, all well and a kicking.

To Mr. & Mrs. Simeon H. Dunham

Bowling Green, Kentucky, November 4, 1862

I now take the present opportunity to write you these few lines to let you know how we are getting along. We are well and can eat two mens rations. This is the first chance we have had to write since you left Crab Orchard. We have Marched about 300 miles. I suppose you herd of the Perryville fight.[26] We was on the battle ground a few days after the fight, it was a horrible site. Our men were well buried but the secesh some were covered with straw some with brush and some was pretended to be buried but thare hands and feat wer sticking out. The town was pretty well riddled, one house I counted 18 cannon ball holes through it. We have not had any rain to amount to anything since we came to Ky., but we had quite a snow storm the 25th of last month. We have got our tents. The report is heare that thare is no fighting for 30 days and the South wanted to settle but we cant believe anything we heare. We expect to get our pay soon. The people think they have hard times in Ill. but let them come down heare and it will cure them. Whareever the army goes they strip evry thing. I have seen a mile of fence laid flat in 15 min. and on fire. Whare we campt at Crab Orchard thare was a farm of 900 acres well fenced and before we left thare was not a rail left on the farm and corn and other things in proportion. A. got a letter from Jane and she said you wer all well. Was out on picket last Sunday. I had to stop writing to go on company drill, but in staid of going on drill they marched the hole company down to the river to wash, I dun up a pile of it to. We are about a half mile from the river. I would not be oblige to live in Ky. if thay would give me the best farm in it, it is all rocks

26. On October 8, Buell finally caught up with Bragg at Perryville and administered a sound beating to the Confederates. A little-known Union Brigadier-General rose to prominence in this battle—Philip Sheridan.

and mountains. The wind is blowing a perfect Hirrycain and to looks like rain. It is getting lait so I ges I will close as I have writen all I can think of. I have comenced at the beegining of the bible and I am a going to read it through. Tel J. Wilson that I will answer his letter soon. Dont wait for us to write, but write as often as you can. Your Afft. Son, Charles L. Dunham.

To Mr. & Mrs. Simeon H. Dunham

Bowling Green, Kentucky, November 4, 1862

As L. has left a small space for me I thought I would fill it out. We are enjoying good health. I weigh 142 lbs., 4 lbs more than I ever weighed before. I wrote E.[ugene] a letter. I suppose he has received it. Will write the rest of the Boys soon. Tell them not to wait for us for our time is so occupied that we do not have but little time to write. I am on guard today at a spring. It is a splendid place. I took a candle and went 70 feet under ground and found water as cold as ice. Ky. is covered with caves and rocks. I must close. A. A. D.

To Jane Dunham

Bowling Green, Kentucky, November 4 and 5, 1862

I suppose you have been looking for a letter from me ere this but we have been marching ever since I wrote that first letter to you. We started from Louisville the next day and have been marching most of the time since. We have been poped through in a hurry. Since we left Louisville, have marched 250 miles. Have not slept under shelter but two nights since we left Louisville. Slept on the ground with nothing but our blankets over us, the earth for a bed. A week ago last sabbath-morning, woke up and found four inches of snow top of our blankets. We have had a very hard time so far, but I gues we will fair better now. We lived on crackers so hard that if we had of loaded our guns with them we could of killed seceshs in a hurry. Day before yesterday we received our tents, and since we camped have had bakers bread and fresh beaf which is quite a treat. Have not received our pay yet but expect to before we leave here. I forgot to say that I had received two letters from you and I received two weeks ago last sunday at 10 o clock at night. Started on a march at 4½ o clock, been going ever since and one last Sabbath. Was very glad to hear from you and to hear that you was enjoying yourself. I am much oblige to mother for that snuff for it came quite handy after marching in the dust all day for it is very dusty here—have not had any rain of importance since last spring. Had an awful time for water the first 4 or 5 days march from Louisville, & has been better since. We have water plenty here river within ¾ of a mile and a spring ½ a mile from camp. Bowling Green is quite a pleasant place situated on the Great Barn River [27] a branch of the Green River. The boys are all well. Mills Louderback, McMurray,[28] & Gregory, received letters from home today. They are as harty as you please. I feel as hearty as a steer in the corn. I can eat all creation of his legs. You must take good care of yourself, and enjoy yourself the best way you can. I would like to be with you and help you make molasses, gather nuts & kind of take a tramp. There is nuts of all kinds here Walnuts, hickery & chesnut. I have a lot in my pocket now. Bill Hallam [29] has been with us two nights. He is as hearty and full of fun as ever. He wanted me to say to you that if you should see his folks to tell them that he was all right side up with care. His Reg.[iment] is camped about a mile from here. Mills has gone over to stay with him tonight. The report is here that the armies are agoing to seace hostilities for 40 days for the South wants to settle. But there is so many reports that we do not know whether it is true or not. If the army keeps

27. Alburtus is referring to the Barren River.

28. Mills Louderback of Company C hailed from Livingston County. He enlisted on August 12, 1862 and was discharged on June 8, 1865 with the rank of sergeant. 2nd Lt. Albert A. McMurray was also a local boy who was eventually promoted to captain on May 1, 1865 and mustered out with the company on June 8, 1865.

29. William H. Hallam, from Livingston County, enlisted on August 21, 1862 and was discharged with his Company C friends on June 8, 1865.

passing through the country as it has done, I dont see what the Inhabitants are a going to do, for I have seen a mile of rail fence destroyed in less than half of an hour. One man had nine hundred acres of good fence as the fence around your pasture and when we left he had not a rail left (I do not see how some of the inhabitants will live until they can raise another crop.) Every thing looks desolate where ever the army has been. Great many of the houses are disturbed and the places are running to rack. People living in the north do not know any more about the hard times the war is creating than a man in the moon. Mills received a letter from the boys at Pontiac last night. They were all right.

Wednesday 5th

Received a letter from you last eve was very glad to hear from you Jane. Do not think that it is negligence on my part for I ment to have written you every week but we have been pushed through so that I have not had time. I have written parts of letters several times and before I could finish it we would have to march. But write often if I dont answer every one in turn. But you may depend upon it that I will write when ever it is in my power. Tell Lydia, not to be scart about my thrashing her for if ever I get home I shall be good natured enough to her, and you to. The opinion of good many here is that we will get home by the first of May or June (I hope so). I forgot to say that I was on the battleground at Perryville, it was a horrable sight. Our men were buried in good style, in separate graves a board at their heads, with the initials of their names on them. But the secesh were buried in all shapes some with their feet out, others with their hands sticking out, one that the hogs had rooted out of the ground and had eaten his brains out and all the flesh to his shoulders. One mans foot and about four inches above his shoe tops where it had been shot off by a cannon ball lying on the top of the grounds. I got some buttons of from a secesh coat that the owner was killed in the battle (I will send you one). Tell Lydia I will write her as soon as possible. I would be glad to receive a letter from her anytime for I presume she has more time to write than I have, for when we are not marching we have to drill so much that our time is most all taken up. Today instead of co. drill we took our bundle of dirty clothes and marched to the River and took the place of wash-woman, came back and went on Brigade Review or Grand Review, as McClellen calls it.[30] I wish you could have been here to off seen it, it is a grand sight. Ephraim Earp[31] was here last night. He has been very sick but is good deal better now. You must excuse mistakes & bad spelling as well as poor writing for I am sitting on the ground my knee for a table which if you try it you will find it rather poor. L. is writing a letter to send home. He says he would like to be there and help you gather nuts, and eat apples. Everything is very high ere especially at the Sutlers.[32] They put on double price cheese 30 cts. per lb., crackers, 7 for 5 cts., Butter in cans holding 1½ [lbs.], $1.00. Other things in accordance. I weighed last night and weighed 142 lbs. more than I ever weighed before. When we left Pontiac I weighed 138 lbs., gained 4 lbs. Love to all save a good share for yourself. Write often, for every letter from you is worth more to me maybe more than you think for. It seams to do all a good deal of good to receive letters. I will write as often as possable. I will close by giving you a diary of our travels since we left Louisville.

I thought I would give you a history of our travels. But it is time to go on dress parade and if I wate shall be to late to get it in the mail in time. I will do it some other time. It is very windy here today, looks like snow growing cold. Dust is flying in to[o]. Everything is covered with dust as you will see by the looks of this paper. I must close so good bye for this time. From A. A. Dunham to his wife Jane Dunham.

Our forces had a fight at Nashville last week captured 300 prisoners, and took a large number of horses & mules, and a large amount of provisions and other stores. The Rebels said that they were willing to go home, for they were tired of it. I am on guard

30. By late 1862 George B. McClellan was better known to Union soldiers for his drilling and parading than for his fighting.

31. Ephraim Earp of Amity Township enlisted on August 5, 1862 and was given a disability discharge on February 20, 1865.

32. A sulter is a person who follows an army and sells provisions to the soldiers.

today at a spring. It is a splendid place. I took a candle and went under ground some 70 feet under ground water as cold as ice. A. A. Dunham. I think of you often.

TO MRS. SARAH J[ANE] DUNHAM [33]

Bowling Green, Kentucky, November 16, 1862

According to promise of writing you every week when I could I take this opportunity. It is very windy today, the dust is flying in torrents, having very pleasant weather otherwise. We are having just such weather as we use to have in Ill., cold and frosty nights but pleasant in the day. We are still camped in the same place we were when I wrote you before but think we will move our quarters nearer town to support the Battery that guards the rail road bridge. Think we will stay there for winter quarters. We just came back from church (as I call it, the heavens for a covering the ground for a seat). Mr. Cotton preached, it was first rate, seamed good deal like home, (but there is no place like home). Took his text from John II Chapter last clause of the 23d verse. There has been about 250,000 soldiers in Bowling Green and its vicinity but good many of them have left for different points. Bill Hallam is with us yet, is trying to get a transfer from his reg. to this, has written to his Capt. but has not received any answer yet. Mr. Gagen,[34] (Editor of the Pontiac *Sentinal*) arrived here yesterday, it is quite a treat for any of us to see any one from Ill. There is a great deal of betting here about the war. Some think it will close soon, others think it will not. We have great many reports but do not know what to believe. And do not have much news otherwise for I have not been ½ mile from the guard line since we came here, only on picket, so you may know that I do not know much about what is going on around us. I have attended two prayer meetings last

33. Sarah Jane is the full name of Alburtus's wife Jane Dunham.

34. William Gagan started publishing the Pontiac *Sentinal* with Philip Cook in 1858. The paper was founded as the Republican opposition to the Livingston *County News*.

week, and heard a sermon today, and expect to attend another this evening. But it does not seam like old times on Scattering Creek when I use to be tramping around with you. I had a dream last night but it turned out about like all other dreams. I went from Pontiac to fathers, got my supper, saddled a horse, and started to go and see my Jane, but when I was crossing the river I awoke. I told forest of it. He said it was a darned shame, and I say so to. He is writing to his Katy darling.[35] Mills Louderback is writing to Mrs. L. I saw Mr. Gregory last eve he told me he was a going to write today to Mrs. G. He is getting very fleshy, McMurray is well. . . . Mr. Howard was very sick when I wrote you before but is a good deal better know, is so as to be around. Bill Hallam is well. E. Earp is getting quite smart. Henry Hayes [36] was quite sick, but I believe is getting better. Ebb Perry [37] was at our tent few evenings ago and he had Margaret Blake's likeness. The report was that they were married. I forgot to say that I received a letter from you the day I mailed one to you, was very glad to hear from you but was sorry to hear that your side troubled you again. I wrote Lydia a letter the next day suppose likely she has received it ere this. I will try and answer Nancys soon.[38] Tell Will I would like to get a letter from him, and let me know how he is getting along. Tell father & mother I would like first rate to be there this winter and help them eat apples, and take a pinch of snuff. That snuff she sent me came in very handy for it was so dusty that some night we looked as if we had been rolling in the road and our throats and head would feel as if they were stopped up. We had a letter from Hercey the same day I got yours. Folks in Ill. will have to look out or they will get a good sousing. There is not much danger of it here at the present time for it has been dry so long that water is very scarce. It was

35. Katie Gurnsey was the sweetheart Laforest left behind in Illinois. They were married shortly after the war and moved to Avoca, Iowa, where they lived for over half a century.

36. Henry Hays hailed from Amity Township and was a soldier in Company C. He enlisted on August 7, 1862 and was discharged on June 8, 1865.

37. Ebenezer Perry was a soldier in Company G and enlisted in Pontiac on August 5, 1862. In November, 1864 he was transferred to another division.

38. Nancy was a younger sister and Will a younger brother of Jane Dunham.

rainy last night but I gess it will not last long. I go on guard today. I must close for breakfast is ready and I go on guard at 8 o clock. I have just finished my breakfast, and the postmaster is calling for the letters and I have to get letters to you mailed on Monday or you will not get it until it has lain in the office in P.[ontiac] for a week. Laforest is detailed for wood chopper today, good bye. Write often. As ever I remain yours, Alburtus A. Dunham.

To Mrs. Simeon H. Dunham

Bowling Green, Kentucky, November 18, 1862

I take this opportunity to inform you that we are still in the land of the living and as harty as two bucks. I received Herceys letter last eve. L. was on picket guard about 3 miles from here and did not get to see it until this morning. We were very glad to hear from you to hear that you were all well, (for it makes any one feel a good deal better to hear from home often). Hercey said you had not received any letters from us since we left Crab Orchard. We have written 3 since then. I received 4 letters from Jane stateing that she had not received any letter since we left Louisville. I had written her 3 or 4 times. We intended to have written so that you and Jane would have received a letter every week. But after leaveing Crab Orchard, we were marched so hard that we did not have time to write to anyone. Hiram thought he would like soldering, but if he had off been along he would have been in the hospital very likely. I use to think I was tired when I had worked all day in the harvest field but I knew nothing about it. The hard march you spoke of from L.[ouisville], we and 5 or 6 of our co. went through but it was hard trying. They were scattered along the road for miles from 2 to 20 in a place just as they gave out. It was a shame the way they marched us. We have marched very hard since, slept on the ground all of the time, never have slept under a roof but 3 or 4 nights since we left home. L.[aforest] & I sleep together. Put one blanket on the ground the other on our coats top.

Sunday morning the 25th of Oct. woke up and found ourselves

covered with 4 in. of snow, it disappeared in 24 hours. Have had very good weather since until yesterday. It commenced raining and rained most of the time until 3 o'clock this afternoon. It has been very dry here for 4 or 5 days so that we were troubled for water. But we are fairing a good deal better now. We have got all our tents within half mile of Big Barren River, a branch of the Green. (you can find it on your map) think we will stay here all winter. I am tonight in a better place than common—at a private mansion ½ [mile] from camp, sitting up with Lieut. Kyle. He has been very sick with the Tiphoid Fever, but it is a good deal better. "I expect you are all abed before this time snooring like good fellows. Levi Whitson [39] is with me." He said you [had] a good lot of molasses, supposed we had plenty. We get a table spoonful about once a week that is not fit for a hog to lap. Have not tasted of butter but once or twice since we left P. and nothing but hard tack until we came here. We have light bread most of the time now. Take the bread in one hand cup of coffee in the other, chunk of fat pork top of that, and then make out your meal. The boys are all well that you know. Henry Hays has been very sick but is a good deal better. Mr. Gregery is as fat as a hog. One of Hoskins [40] men died today, he was in the hospital in town. Mr. Howard has been very sick but is with us now. Men that were very rugged at home are just the one's to be sick here. I was not well when we left L.[ouisville], but thought I would try it and came through at the top of the heap. I weigh 142 lbs. 4 more than I ever weighed before. Have not shaved my upper lip since I left Pontiac, the rest of my face only twice, look some like a wooly dog. L.[aforest] is as fat as a moose. It is the general opinion here that we will be at home by the first of June, but there is so many reports that we do not know what to depend upon. Gen. Rosecrans [41] was here the

39. Levi H. Whitson was a private in Company C from Livingston County. He enlisted in the service on August 14, 1862 and was discharged on April 12, 1865.

40. This reference is to Captain John A. Hoskins of Company A. Hoskins hailed from Pontiac Township and enlisted in the service on September 8, 1862. On June 8, 1865 he was promoted to the rank of major.

41. General William S. Rosecrans succeeded Buell in Kentucky after gaining importance by successfully attacking the Confederates at Iuka, Mississippi.

other day inspecting our arms. You can see his portrait in *Harpers*,[42] it looks good deal like him. He is in Buell's place. One of our men was taken down with the measels today. H.[ercey] said in her other letter something about my not sending my likeness when L. did. I was sick at that time and have not had a chance since, will do so as soon as possable. Have not been paid off yet will send some money home as soon as we get it. We are camped on Mr. Woodruff's farm (he is minister and the secesh burnt his house down last winter, it was a splendid place). The best part of B.[owling] Green was burnt to the ground. I have seen whole towns that were burnt by the rebels. As soon as I can I will give you a history of our travels. We have to drill so much that we do not have great deal of time, or stand guard. Attended three prayer meetings last week and heard Mr. Cotton "our chaplain" preach last sabbath from John II chapter, last clause of 23 verse. Prayer meeting this eve could not attend. Tell Tom, Jo and the rest of our boys not to wate for us but write. We will write them as soon as possable. I hope H. will have good luck with her school. I sent a letter to Jane last Monday. Did E.[ugene] receive the one I wrote him from C. Orchard? Is he agoing to stay there this winter. If so what is he a going to drive at? Tell H. to go to school and study hard. Have you got through husking yet? I wish we were there to help you. Bill Murfey[43] left his co. and they hade not heard from him since. Gagan arrived here Monday. Maples left here last week for Pontiac. Much oblige to you for those stamps for L. and I lent most of our money and are about straped. Expect to get our pay soon. My sheet is about full. I will close for this time. Write often and all the news and how everything is getting along even to the cats & dog, hogs and every thing else you can think off. Good bye. As ever I remain your aff. son, Alburtus A. Dunham.

42. This refers to an article and pictures of Rosecrans in *Harper's Weekly*.
43. Private William Murphy from Sunbury Township was in Company G. He enlisted on August 9, 1862 and deserted on November 3 of that year.

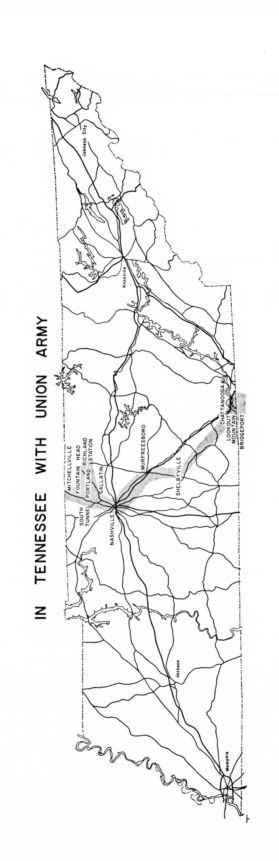

IN TENNESSEE WITH UNION ARMY

The Tennessee Letters
November 24, 1862–May 1, 1864

To Sarah Jane Dunham

Mitchellville, Tennessee, November 24, 1862

In my other letter I told you that we expected to stay at Bowling-Green but instead of staying had marching orders to go to Mitchellsville, Tenn. to guard the raol road at that place. Arrived here after two days marching a distance of 35 miles, passed Franklin and Woodburn very pleasant country from Bowling-Green. Was on lost River, or Mill Cave, as some call it, (a river about 40 miles long) and at this place goes into a cave and runs 5 miles under ground. Laforest & I took a candle and went about a mile into the cave, took about two hours. It was as dark as midnight all the way, very rocky and rough. Use to be a mill at this place but was taken away. It was the place that Daniel Boone, shot the two Indians whilst they were looking over the precipice. Kentucky is the graitest country I ever saw for caves & rocks. I got [in] about half hour ago from town; sold some coffee, that our mess saved, and bought some pies and apples. Pies at 10 cts. apiece. Apples 4 for 10 cts., Coffee 25 cts., corn 50¢ bu., corn meal 50[¢ a bu.] beans $2.50 to $3.00 bu., apples $7.50 per barrell, cheese 25¢ pd. Hard to get at that. I wish I could be with you as I use to last winter and eat some of your apples, as well as to see you and the rest of the folks. We were about ¾ of a mile from the Ky. line in Tenn. Morgan[1] and his band is prowling through this part of the country most of the time for the last month. Our cavelry had a fight with his last week and took 50 prisoners, horses, some cannon & lots of other stuff. Our picks bring in prisoners most every day. We have to be very particular where we go here for his cavelry is lurking around all of the time. When we go after water, or to wash our clothes, some of us have to take our guns and stand sentinal whilst the rest do the work. It is very unpleasant. Mills, Bill Hallam, Howard, McMurray,[2] Gregory are all well. When we left Bowling-Green, we left

1. Colonel John H. Morgan—soon to be a brigadier general in December, 1862—led famous raids into Tennessee and Kentucky.

2. 2nd Lt. Albert A. McMurray was another young man from Livingston County. He enlisted on December 1, 1862, was promoted to Captain on May 1, 1865, and was mustered out of the service on June 8, 1865.

some there sick. Got the news yesterday that our orderly Segt. George W. Yagley[3] was dead. And one of the privates Charles Spencer[4] of five mile grove and Lieut. Kyle they did not think would live. They will all be missed a great deal. Bob Edgerton[5] is sick, good many are having the measles. Ebb Perry just came in to our tent as hearty as ever. Ephram Earp[6] is getting quite smart. Henry Hays rather under the weather is able to be around, but not able to do duty. Henry Hallam was on guard last night, is as hearty as ever. I attended a prayer meeting last evening, expect to attend a temperence meeting this evening. The cause needs to be agitated in the army for there is great many that never drank a drop at home will return tipplers, if they stay long. There is considerable talk here about the war being settled when Congress setts. I hope it will be so. If it is not settled soon I should think they would starve for I have seen farm after farm stripped of every rail on it and house after house disurted. We camped on a farm of nine hundred acres and before we left there was not a rail left on it, and it was fenced with a seven rail fence besides crop fences. If the war should stop now the states of Ky. & Tenn. will not get over the effect of it whilst this generation lasts, if it ever does. We do not have much news to write. I have written every week since we landed in Bowling-Green, have received 2 letters from you in that time. Please write often. You do not know how much good it does a person to receive a letter from one that he thinks a good deal off. I will close. L. says he will fill the rest of the sheet. Good Bye. As ever I remain yours, Alburtus A. Dunham, Love to all, save a good share for yourself.

3. George W. Yeagly was the 1st Sergeant of Company C. He enlisted on August 9 of 1862 and died on November 24 of that year.

4. Charles Spencer was a private from Nevada Township. He enlisted on August 8, 1862, served as a corporal in Company C, and died on November 25, 1862.

5. 1st Lt. Robert P. Edginton from Rook's Creek Township, Livingston County, enlisted on September 8, 1862, served as one of the ranking officers in Company C, and was discharged with his men on June 8, 1865.

6. Private Ephraim Earp was one of Alburtus's dearest friends in Company C. He hailed from Amity Township and enlisted on August 5, 1862. Ephraim was discharged as a disabled soldier on February 20, 1865.

Dear Sister,

As A. was writing I thought I would drop you a few lines to let you know that I am alive and in the land of the living. We have been on the go ever since we left Louisville, but we stood it very well. A. is getting as fat as a pig, tell Will he must take good care of himself. give my love to all. C. L. Dunham

To Mr. Simeon H. Dunham

Mitchellville, Tennessee, November 26 and 27, 1862

I take this opportunity to inform you that we are in *Dixie* and as hearty as *you* please. The last letter I wrote you was from *Bowling-Green*. We then expected to Winter there, but got orders to come to this place to guard the *Rail-Road*. After two days march arrived at the place where we are now camped expect to stay for Winter quarters. "But every thing in the *War* line is so unsurtain, that we cannot tell for any surtainty, may have orders one day to stay, another to march." The first night we camped after leaving B. G. we camped on lost river 3 miles from B. G. where the river goes under ground. L. & I took a candle and went about 1 mile under ground, is a great curiosity. It is the place that Daniel Boone shot the Indians whilest they were looking over the precipice. "I should think it was 50 feet high." The river is about 40 miles long. At this place it goes under ground, runs 5 miles, then emptys into the Green River. It is called mill-cave "at this place," because there was a mill there. It is taken away now. We are in Tenn. ¼ of a mile from the Ky. line. Have to be very careful where we go, for Morgans Cavelry is runing through the country taking all the prisoners they can. Sunday our cavelry took 64 prisoners, 600 head of cattle, and lots of provisions. All of the prisoners I ever saw are very poorly dressed, and most of them look as if they were forsaken. The country from B. Green to this place is a good farming country. The rest of the country we have traveled through is very rocky, and mountainus. Just been to a funeral. A soldier in the 21st Wis.[consin] Reg. was buried about 20 rods from our tent. Has been 5 or 6 deaths in the Reg. Our orderly George W. Yeagly died last Sunday, Lieut. Kyle was left at B. Green very sick, heard since that they did not think he would live. Several complaining.

Dave Finley, A. Ross, E. Schlousher, John Akens,[7] D. Howard—cavelry just brought in 16 prisoners—as well as usual. I have to go on Picket guard to night. Fine weather, quite cold and frosty nights. Thursday 27. Did not have time to finish this yesterday. Today is Thanksgiving wish I was with you to enjoy it. Just recd. a letter from Jane & Lydia, was glad to hear that she was enjoying good health. When I was on Picket I went to a house to get my canteen filled. They asked me to stay to breakfast, did so, had a first rate one. The first time I sit down to a table since we left Louisville. The country here is full of Rebels have to keep close. Part of the rail Road track was torn up 4 miles from here. Had a fight at the tunnel about 8 miles from here. Had to keep very strong guard. Do not known but what they may attack us any time for there is large amount of Provisions here to supply the army at Nashville, and they have threatened to burn them. We are on the N. & L., road. Has been so that the cars could not run through until last week. But when they had the fight tore up the track again.

We do not have much news to write because we have written every week since we landed at Bowling Green, home and to Jane. I hope this war will close soon, so that we shall come home by spring and go to farming. We recd. those stamps H. sent. Would like it if you would send a few more because we cannot get them here, if we had the money. L. & I lent about $12.00 expecting to get our pay before this, so that we are strapped. Everything is very high here. Coffee 30 cts. per lb., corn 50 per bu., meal 75 per bu., apples 4 for 10 cts. or $4.00 per bu., sugar 25 per lb., and everything in

7. John W. C. Akers was a private in Company C and a friend of the Dunham brothers from Livingston County. John enlisted on August 12, 1862 and was discharged with the rest of the men on June 8, 1865.

accordance and hard work for citizens to get them at that. I must close so that L. can put in a few words. Good bye to all. Write often and all the news. From your son, Alburtus A. Dunham.

Dear Father, Mother, Sister & brother

I now take my pen in hand to let you know that I have not forgotten you all yet. Would that I could see you all once again. I was on gard last night and we all had our guns loaded, thare was considerable fireing along the picket line last nite. I did not find out what it was but I guess it did not amount to much. Thare is to companys a going to Nashville to nite to gard a train. We dont know yet whether we will go yet. Hiram be kind to your father and mother and help them all you can and you never will be sorry for it. You dont know how glad I was to heare that you got the house plasterd so that you will all be comfortable this winter. I must close with these few lines, write often. Charles L. Dunham.

I forgot to ask you if E.[ugene] was there yet. The rason I ask is that Mr. Gregory got a letter from his wife. She said she had to draw her own coal which was to much of a job. He said that if he [Eugene] would draw 2 or 3 loads for her he would pay him what ever it was worth. He could get Gregory's wagon if he wanted to draw with. If Mrs. Gregory should not have enough to pay him [Eugene] in full, he [Mr. Gregory] will send it to him. Mr. Gregory sends his best respects to all. Jane wrote me in her last letter that she was agoing to be thare to stay a week or two. Hope she will enjoy herself. C. Spencer, one of our Co., we heard last nite was dead & burried—several others quite sick.

Hope this war will soon end so that we can get home. E. Schlosher is sick this morning. Prayer meeting night before last having temperance meeting here. Some that never drank at home will drink here. I sent you a book more than a month ago, "Dady Horse Doctor." [8] Did you receive it? If so please let me know, from your son, A. A. Dunham.

P.S. Did not get this finished in time to get it in the office. So I will

8. The book mentioned is George H. Dadd, *Modern Horse Doctor*. It was published by Jewett & Company in 1854.

finish this sheet. L. has been after water, just got back. Night before last one of our Company shot at a man supposed to be a rebel spy. Light flurry of snow last night, very cool—that book I spoke of was one I took from a secesh house that was pillaged on our first march to Shelbyville. I did not pay the postage on it, for our post master did not know how much it would be. I will close so, good bye, from your son.

Dear Mother

Burt has written, I thought I would write you a few lines to let you know how I am a getting long. I am well and harty as ever. John Akers and myself went to a barn to sleep last nite. We got back a few minuts ago. It is the opinion of mose evry one that we will be back by spring. For my part I am ready for home any time. Tell the truth I never new what home was till now. It is time the leter was in the office so I will close. Give my love to all and save a good lot for yourself. C. L. Dunham.

To Mr. & Mrs. Simeon H. Dunham

Mitchellville, Tennessee, December 14 and 15, 1862

As I have a few lesure moments I would drop you a few lines to let you know how things are a going. I have [been] so buisy that I have not had time to write. We have been a fortifing nite and day but I have not had any of it to do. Burt has ben very sick for about a weak and I am takeing care of him. He is getting better. Now the doctor sais he will get well rite a long. I am as well as ever. Our Regiment is divided in to 3 different parts and placed a long the Rail road. I wrote this much yester day afternoon. Burt is still getting better. Mr. Gregory wrote to his wife that Burt would not live and told her to tell Jane how it was. If you see Jane you can tel her that he is going to get well. I will write to her soon. The mail is a going to start out soon, and another thing I am so sleepy that I can hardly write. I have not sleep much for a weak. I will write a way again. So good by. Your affectionat son, C. L. Dunham.

To Mr. Simeon H. Dunham

Mitchellville, Tennessee, December 23, 1862

I received your letter yesterday dated the 13 of Dec. and was glad to hear that you are all well. Our Regiment left heare last Saturday and went about nine miles further south to guard a tank. Burt is one of the number. He has been very sick but is getting better. The Doctor said he will get along. I am a taking care of him. He has ben sick about 2 weaks. I received the Pontiac *Sentinal* that H. sent us. It seemed like old. Sunday after the Regiment left thare was any amount of sitisens theare holering for Jeff. Davice. Thar is some good Union people heare. Thare is one good old lady that brings something in every day for the sick. I got the two dollars you sent us and it came in good play for we was compleatly strapt. We did not spend all we brought with us. We lent full half of it to the boys. We think we will draw our pay soon, but we don't know any thing heare for surtin. A soldier don't know what will hapen from one hours end to an nother. You need not send any more money till you heare from me again. Burt will very likely come home as soon as he gets well enough. We have had splendid weather heare all the time. Just about summer weather as our Ingin sumers are in Ill. till now, it is a raining at a two forty rait. The 104 Ill. Reg. was one of them that old Morgan took. He parolled all of them. They went along heare about a weak afterwards on the cars. Ed. Frobrige, Dunham's husband,[9] he had too balls put through his coat. The Ohio boys came up in to line of battle and fired one round and then run. I heard one of the offisers say that our boys fought like tigers. Thay ar expecting a hevy battle in Nashville. Soon the rebels burnt three suttles [*sic*] [sutler's] nite before last on the pike about a mile from this place. Old Morgan is said to be at Cave Sity. Tenisee is the most desolate looking place I ever see.

[Written as a note attached to the foregoing letter] December 29, 1862

9. Sergeant Edward J. Trobridge from Ottawa, Illinois is the young man in question. He was a member of the Ill. 104th, Company A. He entered the service on July 23, 1862, rose to sergeant, was busted back to private, and was discharged with the latter rank on June 6, 1865.

Commenced writing this letter the 23 and the news came that the male was not runing. Come to find out the rebels had tore up the track at Glasgo[w], Ky. They had a pretty good brush. As near as I can learn, our men came out best. Bert is stile on the gain. He sends his love to all you, said we must ceap a stiff upper lip. If a person did not he would not live long. I can't think of any thing more now so I will close, Your Afft. Son, C. L. Dunham.

To Mr. & Mrs. Simeon H. Dunham

Fountain Head, Tennessee, January 7, 1863

I take this present opportunity to drop you a few lines to let you know how we are a getting along. Burt seams to be a bout the saim, not any worse nor much better. He is a good deal better than he was at first but seams to be at a stand now. The rebels tore up the track so we have not had any mail for over 3 weeks nor we could not send any. I under stood this morning that the post master was a going to Louisville to see a bout the mail. Thare has ben some hard fiting below nashville that is about 30 miles from heare. Old Rosencrans has moved them rite and left. We have moved from Mitchellsville. We are now at Fountainhead. I must close with these few lines, for I am a fraid I wont be in time. See Jane if you can and tel her that burt is coming out rite. Your Afft son, love to all, C. L. Dunham.

To Father, Mother, Sister and Brothers

Fountain Head, Tennessee, January 10, 1863

I take my pen in hand to write you the painful news of the death of dear Alburtus. He died Jan. the 7 about 4 o'clock in the afternoon. He was out of his head most of the time during his sickness. When he was in his write mind he wanted me to read the Bible to him. He is buried in the Old Methodist burying ground whare the first confrence Meating was heald west of the Mountains. It is a romantic looking place. The boys in the company got a nice hed board and set out to nice cedar treas, one at the head and one at the foot, and Delos Robinson and myself made a fence around it. His sickness was Brain fever.[10] I will not write any more this time for I cant think of any thing. Pen can not discribe my fealings. Soon as you get this answer it write away. I will write more the next time. We have not had any mail for a month. I will close for this time. Your afft. son, C. L. Dunham.

To Mrs. Simeon H. Dunham

Fountain Head, Tennessee, January 26, 1863

I received your letter of the 27th. Words can not tell you how glad I was to hear from you all and to know you are well all thou it was a long time a comeing. I got it Sunday eav the 11th but Dear Brother was in his grave. You can forme none idea how it seams to me for fears you will not get my last letter I wrote saying about brothers death, so I will speak of it again. He died the 7th about fore o clock in the afternoon. I wrote you a letter the same morning stating that hee was some better. He seamed to be better an till about noon. Then he was dorment but I did not think of his dying. First I new of it, I was [on] one side of the room and he gave to groans and I went to him and he was dying. He did not say any thing he went off very easy. I received your letter of the 3, day before yesterday. I should have written the next day but I went out on a scouting expeditioun and yesterday Sunday we wer inspected by General Pains [11] staff. I was on picket line last nite. You wanted to know if we was clothed worm. We have plenty of clothes and a plenty to eat, such as it is that is hard tack (crackers) and sow bely as we call it. It has been very bad weather heare for some time not very cold but a good deal of rain. One time thare was about 5 inches of snow. The people say they cant recollect when thay had

10. Alburtus died of encephalitis.

11. Laforest is referring to Brigadier General Charles J. Paine of the U.S. Volunteers.

ACTIVITIES NORTHERN TENNESSEE

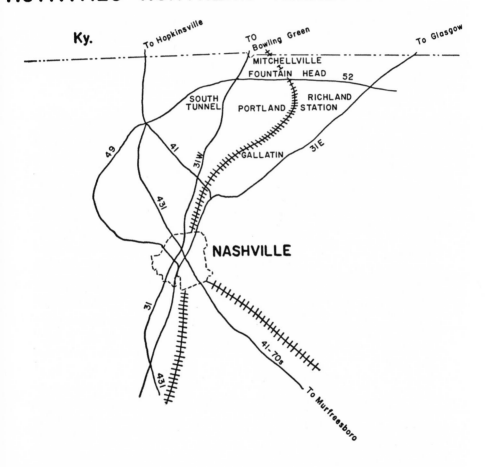

so much at a time. We are taking prisoners almost every day—thare is a good many of old Morgans men disserting and coming to us and taking the oath. Thay say if thay keep leaving as thay have done he wont have any men in a little while. Frank Streamer [12] of Co. A and four others have disserted. Thay had a row with the Captain so thay struck out. All the boys are well that you know. The boys I say for we are all boys heare. I way 146½ lbs. I will close with these few lines hoping thay will find you all well. We are out of ink and cant get any. Love to all, C. L. Dunham.

To Miss Hercey Dunham

South Tunnel, Tennessee, February 7, 1863

I take my pen in hand to drop you a few lines to let you all know how I am getting along. I am well and harty as ever. I hope these few lines will find all of you the same. We are having very cold wether heare now. I dont se but it is as cold as it is in Ill. only it dont last so long. We left Fountain Head last Munday for this place & it is all mountains. It is the most lonesome looking place I ever was in. I received those mittens that ma sent on. Dear Mother you have know idea how glad I was to know that I had got a pare of mitens from home. I received the 5$ that pa sent me. We have not received any pay yet. The report is that we will be paid in a few days, but I shant believe it till I see it. We are a going to draw some more close Munday, thay are hear all redy. Dave Finley has the lung fever, he is at Salitan [13] that is about 7 miles from heare. I have not seen him for about a weak. The rest of the boys are all well that you know. You wanted me to write the particulars about Dear Alburtus. He did not say any think about dying. He was out of his head pretty much of the time. He'd talk a good deal about home in his sleap. One morning he cald me to him and he said that

12. Frank M. Streamer of Pontiac was a sergeant in Company A. He enlisted on August 2, 1862 and deserted on January 26, 1863.

13. Finley's "lung fever" could have been pneumonia or tuberculosis; the term is used for both illnesses. In this case, it is used for pneumonia. Also, "Salitan" is a misspelling of Gallatin, Tennessee.

Hercey & Jane was heare last nite. He thought he was at home most of the time. He is burried northwest of Fountain Head that is about 7 miles south of Mitchellville. Mr. Cotton our Chapplin is a going home as soon as we get paid and I will send A's things home by him. I must tell you of the smal adventur I had day before yesterday. Firs place I am a cavelry man; thare was 30 men detail out of the regiment for scouts. I hapened to be one of them. Thare was 18 of us went as guards for the teams at Mitchellville after the battle, and we run on to a nest of rebels of about a 100, thay was riden long the railroad. They tore up one rail and cut both of the telegraph wires. Thare aim was to captur a train of horses that was a going down. First place we only see one he was wriding down the track. It was write by a cut through a hill. He had a sitizen going along on the side of the track that we was on to tell them if any one was coming. We ordered the sitizens to halt and he stopd. We asked him where he was agoing. Just then we see the rebel. We ordered him [the rebel] to stop and he put spurs to his horse and lunged into the bushes. We was ordered to dismount and by that time he was in the bushes whare we could not see him. He was drest in our close. In a few minuts thare was about a dozen came in plane lite but our commander did not order us to fire. Our head commander was back with the rear guard. We went back for him and the rest of the guard. About that time thay all broke and run. When the rest of the boys come up we took after them and run them about 9 miles. Thay let 8 prisoners go that thay had taken, too of our men and 6 sitizens. We had the range write through the timbers shouting, the snow flew for surtain. Thare wasnt but too shots fired. They were fired at the lieutenant, but thay did not hit him. I will close for this time. Your afft brother, C. L. Dunham.

To Mrs. Simeon H. Dunham

South Tunnel, Tennessee, February 20, 1863

I now take my pen in hand to let you now that I have not forgotten you and am yet in the land of the living all though death seems to stare a person in the fase. We have just lost one of our boys; he was a good boy to. Taint any one you know. I received your letter and package that you sent by Park Lonmice.[14] He arrived heare the 10. Gagan had not left when P. arived heare but then started in a few days after. He did not let any one know that he was a going to Ill. at tall. He slipt of[f] so to get rid of carying any letters or any thing else. I have not received any letter from any of you since that you sent by Park. I received that one you sent with the gloves in. I got a letter from about all of Mr. Guernseys folks from Mr. G. to. He sent me four post stamps. D. Robinson is not very well, J. Nooks[15] is quite sick. D. Finley is getting better. Our First Lieutenant Edgerton got thrown from his horse and was prety bad hurt. I am out scoutting about all the time. We get our meals out in the country. We march up to a house an order them to get our diner or what ever it is and thay get up and dust. The folks look as if thay was all most scart to death when we ride along. I was under the wether a few days back but I ahm pretty smart now. O would that I was at home. I use to talk about being away from home when I was thare but little did I know what it was till now. I hope this war will close soon, but it looks dark to me. You may think I am home sick the way I write, if you do you will think write. I have often drempt that I was at home and how nice it was, but lo and behold when I wake up I am in this blame old tent. I will close with these few lines. Love to all, bushels of it to you. We will muster in a few days a for pay and then we will have six months pay dew us, your loveing son, Laforest.

To Mr. Simeon H. Dunham

South Tunnel, Tennessee, February 25, 1863

I take my pen in hand to drop you a few lines to let you know that I am well and hoping these few lines will find you all the same.

14. No reference was found to the identity of this young man.
15. Jesse B. Nokes was a private in Company C from Livingston County. He enlisted in the service on August 6, 1862 and died on July 31, 1863.

I have ben waiting some time for to send this descriptive letter by some body so have wated longer than I should so I thought I would risk it by mail. You will haf to get some lawyer to get his [Alburtus] pay and bounty. Dave Finley is a geting better, all the rest of the boys are pretty well. I received a leter from Ma and H. the 22 (Sunday). I had just came in from a scout. We took a lot of lether from a secesh but we did not get him. Thare was 6 shots fired out on the picket line this morning. We wer all drawn out in line of battle, it was some of the ofisers. They done it to see how soon we could get out. Thar was some scratching gravel you beter believe. Mr. Gregory is quite sick. Nothing more that I can think of now so I will close. Love to all. Write as often as you can for you can't think how much good it does me to get a leter from home. Laforest.

To Mr. and Mrs. Simeon H. Dunham, Sister and Brothers

South Tunnel, Tennessee, February 28, 1863

I received your letter dated the 21 yesterday afternoon. You can't think how much good it done me. I can look back and see you all thare siting around the stove, Ma busy at work. It seams as if I could see Hiram and Joseph [16] around the barn. He is a whiseling, but little can you think how it looks heare. It is the most misirable plase that man ever see. I will tell you how it is in the tent. J. Marks [17] has popt a lot of corns, most of the boys are a grinding thare teeth on it. One holers, "come Charley have some corns." I go by the name of Charley pretty much all the time. Delos is a writting to his wife & Ross is buisy a grind corn. D. Finley is a getting better, but is not with the regiment, but will soon be. I

16. Joseph was a part-time hired hand on the Dunham farm.
17. Laforest's spelling went awry when attempting this name. The reference is to John Martin, a corporal in Company C from Livingston County. John enlisted on August 5, 1862 and was discharged with the other men on June 8, 1865.

understand that Mr. Boxel is down at Galiton [*sic*] [Gallatin] and Henry [18] is about to get his discharge. He has ben sick for some time. Mr. Houchins [19] was heare the other day. He came down to see his son. He said he see E. [ugene] the day he came to Pontiac to start down heare. Dont wary about me. I may be for the best if it falls my lot to never see you on earth. I hope we will meat in heaven. If you wanted to know if I was to be a cavelry man all the time, I expect we will be; yesterday we drawd a new equipment. Thare is going to be enough mounted to a mount to 100. As I comenced this leter we had just got doen mustering for pay as we have six months pay dew. Will close with these few lines, bushels of love to you all, Laforest.

To Miss Hercey Dunham

South Tunnel, Tennessee, March 8, 1863

Once a gain I take my pen in hand to let you know how I am a getting along a way down heare in the wilderness. I am prety well all though I have ben under the weather for a few days back, but I am comeing out all rite now. I have not got a leter from any of you since last Sunday. We got in from a scout yesterday. We was out about a weak. We captured the notoerious rebel gurrillas. We rode 3 days and nites without stopping only to feud be fore we captured them. We caught them about nine o clock in the evening. [As] good luck would have it thare was none blud shed. We was about 20 miles from camp. We went in that nite. We had to go all the way through the timber (for it is all timber heare). We were looking for the flash of muscetry every minute but they did not molest us. Thare was heavy cannonadeing yesterday southeast of heare. We don't now what it was but we supose it was

18. Henry J. Boxwell was a private in Company G from Livingston County. He enlisted on August 5, 1862 and died at Gallatin, Tennessee on March 3, 1863.
19. No record was found of a Mr. Houchins in Livingston County.

fitting at Franklin, Tenn. or Spring Hill.[20] Mr. Gregory has ben very sick but is getting beter. I believe Finly is getting well; all the rest of the boys are well. H. Boxwell is dead. Mr. B was heare but I did not see him. The order was red to the regiment on deesperrade [*sic*] [dress parade] that all soldiers that can be trusted to come back again can have furlowes. Thare is five to go out of a company at a time. It is very bad wether heare. Most of the time it raind and haild for surtain last nite. Some time last weak the rebels captured a train of cars loded with muels. They took a few and then set fire to the train and burnt the rest of some fifty in number that they burnt. They unhitched the engine from the train and throd all the steam on and let it go down the track hoping it would run in to some other train, but it did not. That hapened in Franklin, Ky. that is bout 20 miles from heare. I will close for this time. Love to all, C. L. Dunham.

To Mr. Simeon H. Dunham

South Tunnel, Tennessee, March 14, 1863

I take my pen in hand to let you know how I am getting along. I am harty as ever. I received a leter from you and Ma yesterday dated the first. I got one today from Hercy dated the 7. You spoke of not geting a leter from me for to weaks. I have writen all ways once or twice a weak, if I am in camp and can. I will be shure and write twice a weak. I just got in to camp yesterday. We had ben out four days. We take a good many prisoners every time we go out. We are a going to start out again tomorrow morning. Mr. Gregory has got his discharge. I gess Dave Finley will get his. The rest are all well, I believe. I was out on a scout when Mr. G. went home. I did not know that he had got it untill I came to camp and he had gone. We have not drawd any pay yet. I have plenty of mony yet. If you have mor at home you may

20. I doubt if the bombardment that Laforest heard had anything to do with the fighting around Franklin and Spring Hill to the south. Franklin is fifty or more miles south of South Tunnel and Spring Hill is nine miles beyond Franklin.

bet your boots this chiken will be back thare. I would rather fite
them than to fight the rebels in the South.[21] You spoke about that lot
that A. left. I would like to have it but you can do as you think best
about it. You must not wory about me. I have a plenty to eat and
drink and good cloths. I will close for this time for I can't think of
any more to write. We are having splendid wether now. I got a
leter today from J. Guernsey. I will close for this time hoping these
few lines will find you all well. If it wasent for breaking the seal I
would get in and come along, C. L. Dunham.

To Mrs. Simeon H. Dunham

South Tunnel, Tennessee, March 18, 1863

  I take my pen in hand to let you know that I have not
forgotten my Dear Ma that yet I am well as I ever was. I have not
much news to write. I maild one Sunday or Munday. I forget
which but I thought a few words would be beter than none. You
said you hoped I would not forme now bad habits. Ma don't let
that wory you any I will not iff not any thing more than for my
Mothers sake. If I do say it forest is a diferent boy since Dear A
died and the thought of home. I hope I shal see you all before long
but if it shoud fall my lot never to I hope we shall all meet in a
beter world whare all is peace. Do not worry about me for I have a
plenty to eat and a plenty of clothse to ware. To be shure we see
some hard times and some good times. The other day I was at
Epersons Sulpher Springs.[22] It was a splendid plase but it has all ben
burnt down since. With in a weak we have captured six wageons

21. This part of the letter becomes confused as Laforest changes subjects.
I would suggest that he is willing to come home and fight the copperheads or
Mother Nature; he expresses such a willingness many times in these letters. From
the general contents of the letter, I would suggest that he is referring to the
latter in this case and expressing his love of the soil and wishing for the challenge
of nature in preference to Southern bullets.

22. Eperson's Sulpher Springs was located twelve miles north of Gallatin or
six miles northeast of South Tunnel, Tennessee. It is now a very small community
known as Sulphura located on the Sulphur Branch of the Dry Fork Creek.

loads of goods such as boots & shoes hats and calico knives and a splendid revolver an a double bored shot gun. One of the boys in Co. J got shot by carlessness yesterday, it shot him through the foot. I gues Dave Finley will get his discharge. D. Robinson is well; Lize Sclosher is fat as a pig; J. Nokes i dont think will stand the show long all though he aint clear down. I guess we will get to months pay tomorrow. I will close for this time for I have run out of any thing more to write, so I will close. Love to all and a write smart for yourself, C. L. Dunham.

TO MISS HERCEY DUNHAM

South Tunnel, Tennessee, March 22, 1863

I received your leter of the tenth ult. Words can not tell how glad I was to hear you was all well. I received your leter Thursday mornin. We was all on our horses redy to start out on a scout as the mail came in. The damn secesh tore up the track again neare Mitchellsville. Co. A & H are stasiond at Richland about a mile from whare they tore up the track. Some of our boys herd the train a coming and all at once they herd a great crash. 40 of our boys grabs there guns and ran up thare and the secesh was plundering the train. Our boys piched in to them and them that see it said they never herd such yeling before. The secesh dropt everything and run. They paid dear for tareing up the track that time for our boys kild one and wonded 7 and taken 17 horses and a lot of guns. None of our boys was hurt. I got a litle a head of my time. We took a number of prisoners thare was some 60 or 70 of the rebels. I had post thare about two ours before the fite. As newse as we could learn [23] they wer hid in the bush. The engine was all stove to peaces. It was a prisonyer train. The ladies waived thare handkerchiefs and cheared our boys on. You wanted to know if I had to stand guard when I was in camp. I have nothing to do only to take care of my horse and when we are out nites we only have an our a peice to

---

23. This confused expression means "as far as we can tell."

stand and some time not that. You wanted to know if I liked it.
Yes, I like it beter than I do staying in camp and I think it is a good
deal helther. If you can read this you will do well. I have sent A's
pocketbook & bible by George Potter.[24] He lives a crost the river.
He will leave them at the post office taint likely they will get thare
as soon as this. I must close so as to get it in to the office so as to hav
it go out this morning. Would that them kisses could be real. I will
close, C. L. Dunham.

To Mr. Hiram Dunham

South Tunnel, Tennessee, March 26, 1863

I take my pen in hand to let you know that I am all rite and
rite on the mix up yet. I received a leter from H. yesterday dated
the 18th. We are having splendid wether heare now. People—what
few are left—are plowing and making garden, peach treas are in
blosum. We are not paid off yet. They say we will be soon and be
paid up to the first of March, but I shant believe it till I see it a
comeing for we cant believe any thing heare unless you know it to
be so. Our scouting [is] dun for a few days. We are expecting an
attact every day. We have to go out about a mile from the regimental picket. Six goes in a squad and stands half of the nite. Thare
is to roads we have to guard. After one squad stands half the nite an
nother comes out and the first one come in. If old Morgan gets
after me and I have to run he will have to get up and dust for I have
got a nag that can just hum now. [You] would think so if you
should see us go once over rocks and logs up hill and down and
every other way you can think. Dave Finley is getting quite smart.
Jesse Nokes I think will get his discharge, if he dont get his
everlasting one before the other is maid out. All the rest of the boys
are well at present excepting bad colds. I will have to close for this
time for I cant think of any thing more. In fact I feal so uneasy I
cant think of anything. I aint contented unless I am on the move all

24. George Potter was a friend of the Dunham family. He was not in any
branch of the service.

the time so I will close for this time and try and do better the next time I rite. Smart heap of love to all, C. L. Dunham.

To Mr. Simeon H. Dunham

South Tunnel, Tennessee, April 1, 1863

Once again I take my pen in hand to let you now I am well. I received your letter of the 20th of last monthe and Ma's, Hercey's & Hiram's of the 26th both at the same time yesterday. I can't think of anything to write for it is the same thing over and over all the time. We moved our position yesterday so that we could hold the plaice beter and not have to put out so many pickets. It is a splendid camping ground. I forgot to tell you that thare was 4 stamps in one of them leters that I got yesterday. J. Nokes is getting beter & Ross is somewhat under the wether but nothing but a cold. I guess all the rest of the boys are well that you know. I should have writen last Sunday but I had not more than got cleand up as I was to do at home, all except poting on my Sunday go to meeting close, than the news came in that thare was some five rebels within about 15 or 20 miles from heare, so we had to strike out. We rode 15 miles in just about an hour. We got in yesterday afternoon. It snowed quite hard heare last nite and froze considerable. It is quite cold to day all though the sun shines. What kind of a hog did my older racer make? I dont suppose I can get a furlow before next fall but I am a going to try. I guess thay will let the married men go first. I got a letter from Tom the other day. I will close for this time for I have run out of anything to write so I close yours, C. L. Dunham.

To Mrs. Simeon H. Dunham and Sister Hercey

Richland, Tennessee, April 12, 1863

I received your leter day before yesterday dated the 3. You cant think how glad I was to hear from you and to know that you was all well. When I hear from you time moves so fast. Just think it is all most a year since I left home but I hope it wont be long before this war will be closed and I will be at home once more. I now what it is to be at home. Morgans men got another good thrashing the other day. Our men took to prisoners and day before yesterday thare was too came and gave themselves up at the tunnel. Our cavalry squad came heare the first of last weak. I dont know how long we will stay heare. Co. A H & F are stationed heare; it is about nine miles from the tunnel. We came heare on the account of saving traveling so far. We wer neaded heare the most. It is splendid wether. The farmers are planting corn. Thare was too boys kild in Co. G. the other day by an accident. One was cleaning his gun and some how his gun went off and shot one through the hart and one through the head, one lived about a minute. The report is heare that Charleston is taken.[25] I hope it is so. If it is so and we whip them down heare [at] Chattano[o]ga, I think thay will have about enough. I think thay will have all the Southern writes they care about. I see Dave Finley the other day, he is prety stout. J. Nokes is about the same. All the rest of the boys are well. H., I received that kiss it was a real one. Would that I could have a real one. Ma you wanted to knowe if I had Sunday to my selfe. Sunday is the same to a soldier as any other day. We are out scouting most every Sunday. We find a good many sparking on Sunday, it makes them get care about them times. We have not got any pay yet but I think we will get it this weak. I cant think of any thing more to write this time so I will close for this time, C. L. Dunham.

To Miss Hercey Dunham

Richland, Tennessee, April 15, 1863

I received your leter some time a go. I should have writen sooner but I am scouting so much that I dont get time to write or

25. On April 7, 1863 Samuel F. DuPont attacked the forts protecting Charleston harbor. Instead of the victory expected—and mentioned in Laforest's letter—the Union squadron was repulsed. Continued efforts to take the forts and Charleston met with the same fate until February, 1865 in Sherman's final campaigns.

anything else. Thar is some 60 mounted men piked [*sic*] [picked]
out of the Regiment on for scoutting. I hapened to be one of them.
We are out some times a weak at a time; we go nite and day. I like it
much better than staying in camp all though we run a good deal of
risk. We hardly ever go out with out caching a number of prisoners or spying out something new. Day befor yester thare was 57
rebels came with [in] about 12 miles of heare to make a raid on the
railroad but we was to sharp for them. We new all about thare
moves. They ran in contact with some of our cavelry that are
stationed at Franklin, Ky. and they fed them some of uncle sams
pils,[26] kild a number of the rebs and took several prisinars. None of
our boys wer hurt. We run our horses to about 15 miles to cut off
thare retreat but they went annother road. We rode all nite after
them but did not get any of them. We are haveing splendid wether
heare. Thare is a going to be a great deal of fruit heare this seson,
peach treas are loded down. That is all this country is fit for just to
rais fruit. Know wonder that this state rebeld. You cant find one in
20 and be safe in saying so thay can read or write. The country is
all rocks and mountains. The union ladies of this state and along the
line of Ky. gave ous a picknick the other day. We had a fine time,
it seamed a good deal like home. I think if nothing happens I will
get a furlow to come home about August. I think we will stay
heare all summer. General Pain sais that this Regiment has done
more good along this road than a briggade had done before. Since
we have ben out we have taken some 1900 prisinors. I will close
with these few lines hopeing to do better the next time. Love to all
and lots for yourselfe, C. L. Dunham.

To Mr. Simeon H. Dunham

South Tunnel, Tennessee, April 16, 1863

I take my pen in hand to let you know that I am well and that
we have drawd our pay. E. Maples is a going to start for Pontiac in

26. Throughout these letters Laforest refers to "Uncle Sam's pills" or "blue
pills." By this phrase he means bullets; sometimes he refers to cannon balls and
various size bullets.

the morning. He is a going to take a lot of muny for the boys. I let him have 40$ for you. He is a going to leave the muny at R. Babcock's the store keepe so you will get it thare. It is about eight o'clock in the eavening. I have ben wriding pretty much all day and it has ben very warm so I am pretty tierd and sleepy but never to tierd to write home. Now something else, how are you getting along with your work? I wish I could be thare to help you but I will help you all I can other ways. We are scouting most all the time. I often thought how it must seam to the soldiers when they was scouting that is when I was at home. A person never knows when they will run on to the enemy. Thare aint any fite in the devils that are prowling a round hear. Fight is not thare mottow, rob steal & tare up the rail road track. If they see half thare equal a comeing every last buger will run for sweet life. I have helpt catch a number of the devels but after this I have maid up my mind when they throw up thare arms and holer dont shot I will never pull my gun down again. I will let them have one of Uncle Sams pills for they are shure cure. I must close for this time. Write as soon as you get the mony sow I will have it on my mind, C. L. Dunham.

To Mrs. Simeon H. Dunham

South Tunnel, Tennessee, April 25, 1863

I have now news to write but I thought I would scribble of a few lines to let you know that I was well and can eat all before me. We are out evry day, evry day I say most evry day. We have ben scouting nites a good deal latily. Thare was 15 rebels rushed in to a union mans house the other day, and shot him through the arm and then took him along with them. We have ben after them ever since but we could not catch them for they had some 7 or 8 ours the start on us. I expect we will try them another pull tonite. It will be a dear pill for them if we ever get hold of them. It is splendid wether heare. The treas are prety much all leaved out. I have seen some corne that was up. I supose Pa has got that money that I sent him before this. It is about nine o clock in the fore non. I expect you are all busy at work. I will lay around all day and travel to nite. We go in squads all through the cuntry and have sertain places to meat. We pick up a good many of the devels. I have bought me a revolver but I aint to pay for it till next pay day. In the business that we are in a person neads one. I received a leter from you and H. a day or too a go dated the 18. As long as I can heare that you all are well at home time slips off smooth. H. said in her leter that A. Foster talked of going as an officer in a negro regiment. Any man that will go in to a negro regiment aint fit to be cald a man. I have seen enough of the baboons since I have ben down heare. I will close with these few lines, a few more words I want to say. Dear mother dont wory about me for I have a plenty to eat & a plenty to ware. I feal as Dear Brother said before he died, sais he Forest if I die heare I die in a good couse. I will close so as to get it to go this morning. Love to all and lots for yourselfe, C. L. Dunham.

To Mr. Simeon H. Dunham

South Tunnel, Tennessee, April 30, 1863

Once again I take this present opportunity to drop you a few lines to let you know that I am well and as harty as a mule. I received your leter last eavning of the 24. I was glad to heare that you was al well and was getting a long so well with your work. We muster again this afternoon for pay. We muster evry too months, this makes six times that we have mustered. 10 months of our time is gon. It dont hardly seam posible but come to look back and see what I have ben through & what I have seen it looks full as long as 10 months. D. Finley is at the regiment; J. Nokes is not well yet but is a getting beter; the rest of the boys are all well I believe. I am at Ritchland Station yet. I think our Regiment will stay along this road all sumer. I got a leter from Jane yesterday. I supose you have hurd all about our Colonels comeing home.[27] The news came yesterday that his resignation was not expected [*sic*] [accepted]. I hope

27. Lt. Colonel Andrew J. Cropsey was the commanding officer of the Illinois 129th. Colonel Cropsey hailed from Fairbury, Illinois. He enlisted on September 8, 1862 and resigned on February 27, 1864. His April, 1863 resignation was not accepted, and he remained in his post for almost another full year.

it is true. A beter man cannot be found to fill that place. The rest of the officers got down on him becase he did not think himselfe enough above the privates, all the privates thought everything of him. Hercy spoke about some things I sent them a month a go by a felow by the name of George Potter, and I sent a leter the same time by maile. He lives on Rooks Criek. I done them all up as if I was going to send them by express & he was to leave them at the post office at Pontiac. I thought about writing several times to about them, but I would forget it evry time I wrote. I will close, C. L. Dunham.

To Mrs. Simeon H. Dunham

Richland Station, Tennessee, May 8, 1863

I received your leter last eavning and candies that you sent by Maples. The mush is just what I wanted I had ben trying to get some for a long time. I am well. We just got in from scout last eavning. Maples had ben heare for two or three days. Thare is too of our boys a going to start home this morning on a sick furlow. Thare is not much prospects of my getting one for a good while unless some of you was sick but I shal try my best. A young felow that is well dont stand much of a chance to go home. I have not time to write any more this time for it is about train time and the boys are a going to start, so good by Ma for this time, C. L. Dunham.

To an Unknown Friend

Richland Station, Tennessee, May 13 and 14, 1863

It is with pleasure that I take this present oportunity to drop you a few lines to let you know that I am a live and cicking. I received your leter some time a go. We are going so much that we have to cach it when ever we can but beter late than never. I am glad to heare that you are haveing a good time for farming this summer. You nede not be much surprised if you should see me thare about harvest.

May 14. I had to stop writing yesterday for we was ordered to sadle up and we was of double quick. Thare was 57 rebels come in to make a rade on the railroad but they could not quite come in. Thay went near Franklin, Ky. that is about 12 miles from heare. Thare is too Co. of cavalry stationed thare and they introduced them to some of uncle sams blue pils. They kild a number of the rebs and put them to flite. We run our horses about 15 miles to cut off thare retreat but they scooted all over the country as they all ways do. We rode all nite but did not run on to any of them. We got in to camp about noon. You can gues about how I feel after riding a day & nite. Enough of that, I must tel you what a fine time we had the other day. The union ladies of this state and along the line of Ky. gave ous a picknick, we had a good time. Thare is some good looking gals down heare, union girls that is. We run in contact with a secesh ladie the other day—I ought not to say ladie about a secesh devel. She cust ous fore & aft bout we have got use to that. Have you ben to any wegen meetings lately? [28] We have preaching heare every Sunday but it is not half of the time that we are in camp to heare it, that is ous mountted men. Now a little about the war. Iff things keep on for two months as they are now, I think it will be closed by this fall. Give my respects to all inquiring friends. I will close with these few lines, love to all, C. L. Dunham.

TO MR. SIMEON H. DUNHAM

Richland Station, Tennessee, May 18, 1863

I have but a little to write but I thought a few lines would be beter than none. I am well and hope these few lines will find you all

28. In this sentence—and on many other occasions in later letters—Laforest refers to "wegen" meetings and "wegen" gals. The word is a local slang expression which refers to the Norwegians and other Scandinavians who live in a portion of Esmen Township. Laforest and the addressee of this letter also lived in Esmen Township. In fact, the Dunham property is very close to the Olson's and other "wegens." The word does not denote contempt or disrespect; rather it is simply a local designation for these people which lasted into the twentieth century. Obviously, many of the "wegen" gals were among the most beautiful in the county.

the same. I am glad to heare that you are having a good time for farming. This summer crops looke very well here, but they dont grow as they do in Ill. The rebels fired too shots at one of the pickets Saturday nite, now one was hurt. Lige Schlosher is prety sick, all the rest of the boys are well. Cropsey is now Liutenant Colonel. I dont know hoo will be major. I had to stop writing and go out an drill. I have just got in. We drill once in a while when we are laying in camp. I have not stood picket for four months. When we are out miles we dont have to stand gard mord than one hour in all nite & some times not that. I will have to close with these few lines for I cant think of anything more. Love to all and rite smart heap of it to, writ as often as you can, C. L. Dunham.

To Miss Hercey Dunham

Richland Station, Tennessee, May 22, 1863

I received your leter of the 16th on the evening of the 19th. We started out on a scout the next morning we got in last evening. I dont knowe what I should do if I was in the fix that some of the secesh are. I was talking with a rebel prisinar that we took the other day & he said he had not hard from home for 17 months. I am glad to heare that you like your school. One of the boys in our Co. broke his arm the other day, he was a guard with the forage train. They had a lode of hay and the wagon felt over & he hit on his arm. Lige Sclosher is a getting better, all the rest of the boys are well. We are a going out scouting again to nite. The last trip we was out we got some 17 horses. The 4 o clock mail train has just gon down. I will have to close with these few lines. I am a shaimd to not write any more but I thought a little would be better than none & that you would know that I am well. Love to all, C. L. Dunham.

To Miss Hercey Dunham

Gallatin, Tennessee, June 5, 1863

I received your & Mas leter of the 26 of last month several days ago. I have ben so buisy ever since that I could not find a chance to write till now. We moved down heare the first day of this month. I was within a few miles of Nashville yesterday. They are a going to get our Regiment togather once more and we will hold this place that is if Morgan dont wipe ous out, but let him come if he thinks best. We will introduce him to some of uncle Sams blue pils. Have you got my picture yet & do you think it looks natshural? I weight more than I ever did. I weigh in my shurt sleaves 145 lbs. I am a going to 150 then stop. We can get ripe cherys heare for 10 cts. a pint, mulberys are plenty when we are riding a round through the woods. We get all them we want. The first Lieutenant of Co. D was kild yesterday by the rebels. That Co. is stationed at Ritchland guarding a bridg whare we left. We have a very nice place heare to stay. Our quarters are in a splendid building that some ritch secesh has left. It looks now as iff we was a going to get some [?]. . . .[29] This town is about the size of Kanka-kee City [Illinois]. All the boys are well I believe. I will close with these fine lines for thare aint any news to write that amounts to any thing, so I will close, C. L. Dunham.

To Mrs. Simeon H. Dunham

Gallatin, Tennessee, June 10 and 11, 1863

I received your & Hercys & Hirams leter the other day. I should answard it sooner but I had writen one & sent it the same day I got your. I am well & harty as ever & as ugly to. Have you got my likeness yet? I like this place very well, but not as well as I do the place we left. My company that is Co. C is Provost guard in town. The company that I am in now is Co. L. Thare is a fare prospect of hole Regiment being mounted. I hope it will. I dont like this marching it is too much pork for a sixpence, & not enough for 5 do. Thare is 150 of ous mounted now. Thare was one of our mounted squad got drownd yesterday. He was in swimming in the cumberland. He did not come up but once. The current was very swift. His body is not found yet. He was a good boy, his loss is felt

29. This portion of the manuscript was almost impossible to read and two words had to be excluded.

very much. His brother is in the same company, they belonged to Co. A. I am glad I have now more brothers in the army. Dear Mother dont wory about me. I hope I will see you all once again before long but litle do we know what will hapen. Life is unsertain heare especily but dont wory about me. I believe I can stand what any one else can. We have a plenty to eat & a plenty to ware. Of corse we see some hard times & good times but it is all in a persons life. It has ben raining very neare all day. I have not got a leter from Eugene yet. I shud write to him in a day or to if I can catch a chance. We are busy most of our time. It is not hard work but we have to do it. Scouting or out post picket duty is not hard. We have only two hours to stand in a nite. I will write Hiram a leter soon. I expect he is sporting some bodys girl before this time, some wegen gal I expect. Whare is Tom & what is he doing? I wrote him a leter some time a go but have not got an answer, also John S. I have not got an answer but I suppose they are busy. What is E.[ugene] driving at in Ind., your leter was dated the 31. I did not get that paper. It aint half of the time that papers wille come through. Did you get that one I sent you? The next time any of you write [tell me] if you are a mind to. I will close for this time. Lots of love to you all & thousands for yourself dear Mother, C. L. Dunham.

June 11. P.S. We was all up last nite expecting to have a little brush down on the river but it did not come off. I forgot to say yesterday that we was paid off again day before yesterday. We was paid 26$. Thare is one months wages back yet, they keep one months back all the time. I shant send any of this home at present unless you want it for it may be that I can get a furlow before long.

To the Family

Gallatin, Tennessee, June 18, 1863

Dear ones at home, one and all. I take this present opportunity to drop you a few lines to let you know that I am well. I got a leter a day or too ago that I did not answer, for I had writen one the day before. It was from Ma. I got one from H. last nite that you sent by

Wilson,[30] it was dated the 10th. Things are about the same as ever. We have ben looking for a fight theare for a number of days but I guess it has plaid out. I guess I never told you that the most of our Regiment was holding a fort. We drawd something like one thousand barrels of water in a day into the fort, there is to large sisterns in it. If they do com we will get in thare & we will give them what a stick give the drum. Thare was now end to the provisions that we had in thare. We prepared for to stand a sige iff we had too. It is quit after two days raining some. George Allen[31] started home yesterday morning on a furlow. I did not know that he was a going till he was gone. I had the promise of one the first of July but they have just a stop giving them to only them that are sick or some one sick at home but I think that will play out soon. I think the reason they did it for they wanted all the able men heare for we would need all the forse thare is heare if we was attacked. I will be thare some time for a great while. I will close for this time for I have writen all I can think of, C. L. Dunham.

To Miss Hercey Dunham

Gallatin, Tennessee, June 21, 1863

I received your & Mas leter yesterday of the 19. I am glad to heare that you was all well. Your leter found me harty as ever. I am glad to heare that your school is so neare out so that you can be home with Ma. I think the war wont last much longer; the head officers think it wont any how. Thare offering to bet a good deal on it and thay are takeing down the number of our guns. I dont see how the secesh can stand it much longer. Any how you cant imagin how things look down here in rebeldom. Pepeal mat [*sic*] [might] think they know a good deal about it by what they

30. Joseph Wilson was a friend back home who made many trips to visit the men in the field.

31. George C. Allen was a friend from Laforest's home township of Esmen and he was in Company G. George enlisted on August 5, 1862 and was discharged on June 8, 1865.

read but come rite down to it they dont know any thing at all how it is. We made a number of them bite the dust & the other day we burnt a lot of houses and distileries. We got in a nest of them so we went to work. You would think all the wild animals in the world was let lose if you had herd the shouting and yelling that was done. The wether is pretty good now but thare has ben so much bad that it may [have] spoilt pretty much all the wheat thare has. A number of sitisens told me that it had grone so in the shock that it was not fit for anything. I had a mes of green corn for dinner. It only cost 10 cts a dosen that is a dosen ears. Potatoes are a doler and a doller & a half a bushel. Whisky the same. The boys are all well. The Regiment is very helthy as a general thing. I will send Pa tenn $ in this leter. Has he got that five I sent? I ges it is about as safe to send it by male as any way. I will close with these few lines, your loving brother, C. L. Dunham.

To Miss Hercey Dunham

Gallatin, Tennessee, June 25, 1863

I received your & J. leter yesterday so I take present opportunity to drop you a few lines. I am well as ever. Peter Loler [32] started home yesterday morning on a furlow, they have commenced giving them the same as ever. I have the promace of one but I dont know how soon I will get it. You need not look for me at all till you see me thare for it is very uncertain. It has ben raining for too days now a very cold rain too. We have ben expecting old Morgan for some days. We have out three lines of pickets one of infantry & two of cavelry. He was within six miles of heare last sunday with five regiments. They wer crossing the river & some of our forces got in behind him & cut him up pretty bad. Iff it hadent ben for that we would had a pull at it. I dont think he will try comeing again very soon.

The cow bel rang so I had to go to dinner & feede my horse.

32. Peter Lawler was a private from Livingston County. He enlisted on August 11, 1862 and was killed in action on May 27, 1864.

Now I will finish—first place I will let you know what I had for dinner. We had fresh beaf boild, bakers bread that we have all the time now & coffee. Ma if you are a mind too you may send me a couple pare of stockings & another box of that ink powderd, lost the other before I had used any of it. Send it by Peter Lawler. I did not know that he was a going for surtain. I was out on picket. I just got in in time too see him start off. I should sent a letter by him if ide had time to writen one. If Pa had the money too spare he can get me one of these ruber blankets soldiers blanket & send [it to me]. He [Peter Lawler] is a going to bring one for [Company] A. boys. Pa if you have not the money so that you can spare it just as well as not let it go for thare will be other chances if I dont get a furlow. If I dont get a furlow I will send you som money soon. We will be paid of the first of next month if nothing hapens. Nothing more at present so I will close with lots of love to all, C. L. Dunham.

TO MRS. SIMEON H. DUNHAM

Gallatin, Tennessee, June 30, 1863

I received your leter last nite. I am glad to heare that you all was well. I have not any use to write of any account. About all I can say is that I am well & harty as ever. We have had rainy bad wether for several days. I will be on rider duty to nite. It has raind so much that the cumberland river is just a turning up. Thare is a fleete a going up tomorrow. I gues they will have a bit of a fight for Old Morgan is just the other side of the river. As long as the river ceeps up he cant get over this side. I presume you have seen Peter Lawler before this. I think if we take Vicksburg I think the war will close in the corse of six months. When we go on rider duty thare is three of ous go together. I was out the other nite and we took a prisinar. He said the head men in the South was giving too dolers of thare money for one of ours. He disseded [*sic*] [deserted]. He said he had not had any thing to eat for six months but meat & bread, now coffee nor sugar tea or anything of the cind. I will have to close with these few lines for I cant think of anything to write. You must not think bad for I will do the best I can so I close, C. L. Dunham.

To Mr. Simeon H. Dunham

Gallatin, Tennessee, July 12, 1863

 I take my pen in hand to drop you a few lines to let you know that I am well. It is some time since I hurd from any of you. I suppose you have hurd about the railroad being tore up & the mail being taken. The trains are running now. I am heare alone most of the boys went out last nite on a scout. They took two peces of artilery with them. They thought they would have a fight this morning & I guess they are having it for we can heare cannonadeing of in the directtion they went. Morgan is in Ind.[iana]. If they let him get out of thare without capturing him I shal think we mite as well give up & done with it. Vicksburg is ours, so far that is encourageing. I got a leter from Eugene & Bill Rockwell [33] yesterday. They was not well when they rote. Are they doing much about the draft thare & what do the people think of it? The bel is ringing uptown for church. Peter Lauler has not got back yet this time was up at 10. I have got a very lame arm, I was vascinated & it took a good hold. Thare was a great cry about the small pox one spel but thare was nothing of it. We have had very bad wether for some time. The cumberland is just a comeing. I use to complain about Illinois but I think I can be satisfied if I ever get back again. We have plenty of aples & blackbery. Berys thare is no end to, peaches are just a turning. I will close with lots of love to you all so good by. I will not put this in the office now for I may get one from some of you to nite when the mail comes in. I got a leter from Ma & H this eve. dated the 8. I am glad to heare that you are all well. I understand tonite that the track is all tore up in Ind. so that this

---

33. William Rockwell was a friend from Esmen Township who had not enlisted in the 129th.

wont be apt to go, but I will post it in the office. It may go, C. L. Dunham.

To Mrs. Simeon H. Dunham

Gallatin, Tennessee, July 17, 1863

I received your leter that you sent to Peter Lawler. I am glad to heare that you are all well. I am well as ever. I have know news to write that amounts to anything. We have had very good wether for a few days but it looks as if it would rain again soon. I got the stockings, towel, and other things that you sent. The stockings and towel was just what I wanted. Peter did not get me a blanket. He said that thare was not any in Chicago nor in Louisville but I think he got on a spree and lost the money or spent it. He sais he had it stole from him but he got some money and gave me the five $. If I get a furlow I can get one then. I dont think I will get one now before August or September. I would send 20 or 28$ home now but if I should get a furlow I will have to cach the chanse. We are a going to have a kind of spree tonite for supper. Some half dosen of ous put in fifty sents a pice and bought a lot of oisters, so you see we will go in on our nurves. This is the greatest place for Black berys that I ever see. We can go out and not be gon but a litle while and get a large pail full. The report is now that general Pain got a telegraph despach that Old Morgan is captured. I hope it is so but I fere not. Things lok prety favorable now. The head men seme to think heare that the war wont last six months longer, but that it could be so. I got a letter from Eugene and Bill the other day, thay was all well then. I will close with these few lines. Love to all and lots for yourself, C. L. Dunham.

To Mr. & Mrs. Simeon H. Dunham

Richland Station, Tennessee, July 28 and 29, 1863

I received your leter of the 20th yesterday. It makes me feel so glad when I get a leter from home [and] heare that you are all well. I can also whip a half dosen secesh about that time. Thare was too of our boys just got back that went home on furlow. We nead raine heare very much. Thare will be know end to the fruit heare this summer. We are a going to get new guns. Our mounted Co. is Co. L, but you can direct your leters the same as you all ways have done. The boys in Regiment are very helthy as a general thing. Lige Sclosher is some what under the wether yet, but I think will be all rite in a few days. About a furlow I dont see much of a site of getting one the way things are a working but I will do what I can to get it. Iff I should be in the share of next winter, Eugene was a mine to come down & stay in my plase for a little while.[34] I could do that way but that is a good ways of. I believe the show will be wound up by next winter. Vicksburg is ours I suppose.

Thursday morn 29th. I stopt writing last evening thought I would finish this morning for it would not go out till morning any how. I have just got done eating my breakfast. We have plenty to eat that is good. It raind pretty hard last nite, it looks as if it was a going to be a rainy day. About that napsack—I tried to turn it over [sell it] but I could not. Thare was not anything else but an over coat & that I sold a few days ago to one of the boys. He is to pay for it next pay day. They say we will be paid off again some time next month. I shant believe it till I se it a comeing. I will close for this time. Love to all lots of it to, C. L. Dunham.

To Mr. Simeon H. Dunham

Gallatin, Tennessee, August 5 and 6, 1863

I received your and Joes leter of the 29 of last month in due time. I am glad to heare that you are getting along so well with your work. It is very nice wether heare but very hot but have a shour every day or so. The health of the boys as a general thing is very good. They all say that I am as fat as ever. J. Nokes died last weak. He had not ben very stout for a long time. He was taken

---

34. It was perfectly acceptable for a friend or a relative, of proper age and physical fitness, to replace a soldier for a short furlough.

down very low and went awl of a sudden. Mr. Howard, the man that use to run Allens saw mill, is a going to start home on a furlow in the morning. I gues he will come and see you. I am having very easy times now. We was up a good deal nites when Old Morgan was neare heare, but he is whare he ought to ben long a go. It don ous good when we found out that he went into Ind. for we was prety sure that he would get all that he bargaind for before he got back and shure he did. All that I regret is that they did not kill the whelp. Thare has been some tall slautering done heare with the rebels. Bush whackers lately. I am a thinking they [bush whackers] will get enough after a while for every one we cach without killing some how dont get into camp. You can juge for yourselfe what becomes of them. It beats all how many thare is a comeing in every day and a takeing the oath. I dont believe that 150 would be as meny that has taken it today, and at Carthage, a place east of heare, they flock in like bees. For my part I think rebeldom has about plade out iff not quite. I got a letter from Hurcy this eavning dated August the 5 but I gues it must have ben July the 5, in fact I know it is the leter reads. You nead not send any blanket now for I dont know but what we will draw them yet. I will close as I have writen all I can think of and it is a getting late. Lots of love to you all.

August 6. Sunday morning. I am well and harty. It is a splendid morning. I would like to be thare to go to meating with you and see you all but that cant be. Know more now so good by, C. L. Dunham.

To Mrs. Simeon H. Dunham

Gallatin, Tennessee, August 17, 1863

I now take my pen in hand to drop you a few lines to let you know how I am getting along. I am well and harty and am haveing easy times which I will tell about pretty soon. It is very warm wether, have a shower every day or two. Time are very still. Now talk of a fight as thare was when old Morgan was around. When he went to Ind. he crost the cumberland not but a litle ways from heare. The guerilias are haveing to walk chalk around heare. Walter Good [35] got back heare last weak Wednesday all rite. He said he told you about my being under arrest. I have not done any duty for about two months and wont for annother one to come for my time wont be up for a month.[36] Good told you all about it so thare is no use of my writing all about it. The sontance was too months pay and hard labor with a ball and chain, but the Colonel would not let it be done. My capten kicked up quite a row about it. If my capten could have ben at the trile they never would have done anything with me at all, but he was detald on som duty & that he could not be there. He and the Colonel went and examened the papers and they said that they had know business to pass any such sentance, but thare is know justice in a cort marshel for a privat. A private is know body anyhow, but evry dog has his day. But the ball and work was with drawn so all I have to do is to eat and take my end, but as to the pay I will draw the to months when I am discharged. I dont suppose I can get a furlow untill this fall. I may get one pretty soon after I get out of heare but cant tell. You must

35. Walter Good of Livingston County was the 1st Sergeant of Company C. He enlisted on August 14, 1862 and was discharged with wounds on November 10, 1864. He was a good friend of the family and carried the distasteful imprisonment news to the Dunhams.

36. Nowhere in this letter, or later ones, does Laforest record the details of his court martial. However, from what was not said and from the character of the young man, I would like to prognosticate what might have happened. Less than two months earlier, Laforest and his fellow soldiers came out of the mountains of Richland Station and South Tunnel to the city of Gallatin. They had not been to town and kicked up their heels for many months. Laforest was a proper young man brought up by a puritanical New England Christian family. I suspect that he took snuff but pursued few other vices before he went off to war. Now he is exposed to prostitutes, whiskey, and the like; and, as happens to a young man away from home for the first time, he experimented a bit with the vices of this life, especially whiskey. I would suggest that Laforest and his fellows visited Gallatin, absorbed a bit too much whiskey, got into a rip-roaring fight and tore up a bit of the town—and each other. Maybe it was Laforest alone for the letters do not indicate that others were involved. I do not think that the court martial was for anything more than excessive drinking, and its results, or something similar. The sentence—and his superiors' reaction—seem to support this supposition.

not wory about me for I am doing first rate. I will close for it is getting late. Lots of love to you all and a write smart chance for yourselfe, so good by, C. L. Dunham.

To All the Family

Nashville, Tennessee, September 4, 1863

I once again take my pen in hand to inform you that I am well though I have lost my strength since I have ben under arrest on the account of not haveing too move around much. We left Gallitan to weaks a go to day for this place. The Regiment marched heare but Delos Robinson & several others and myselfe came on the cars. It was quite a pleasant ride. I received too leters from you yesterday, one of August the 16 and one the 21st. Today I got the letter and paper that you sent by Howard. You may think it strange that I did not get them before so I will tell you I have not ben with the Regiment since we left Gallitan. I am in the guard house yet. I have not sene any of the boys since then untill today. A. Ross came over and see me. The boys came ove a number of times but could not get to see me but A. got a pass from the General to see me. They have any amount of our men prisinors heare, some for one thing and som for another. So you see that they dont let evry one see them. The boys brought Mas leters heare as soon as they came but they did not give them to me heare. My time will be out heare Sunday. I will be all rite before you get this. The Regiment has got new guns. I dont think we will stay heare long, but cant tell what they will do. May take a start all at once and not know whare we are a going till we fesh up. Thare is a good deal of talk about England and France comeing in to help the south but I gues it is all a blow.[37] Rosencrans

37. During the first two years of the Civil War there was considerable concern in the United States that England and France might enter the conflict on the side of the Confederacy. By the time of this letter the "Laird" rams controversy was before the world, and in early September American Minister Charles Francis Adams and British Foreign Minister Lord John Russell were exchanging their famous notes on the subject. The question of possible foreign intervention was one of natural concern to the soldiers in the field.

is moovein forward. They are a scirmishing some evry day, but I dont believe the rebs will stand [and] fite. They are sending the rebels heare by droves evry day and such a raged set of poor devels you never see. I should think they would dissert faster than they do. It is now about supper time. It is very cool wether heare. It is cooler than I ever see it thare this time of the yeare. The soldars are very healthy as a general thing. I cant think of anything more to write so I will close with lots of love. Hi, how is May [38] or havent you seen her lately, C. L. Dunham.

To Miss Hercey Dunham

Nashville, Tennessee, September 14, 1863

I have not much news to write but a few words may be better than non. I am well and hope these lines will find you all the same. When I know that you are all well at home time slips off fast let hapen what will. I received two leters from you last eavening, one was dated september first and the other the 8th. You beter believe that I was all rite when I got them. Those few lines of print that Ma sent is true evry word of it. Litle did I know what home was or how to prise it till I came into the army. Would that evry boy knew what I know now. They never would speak a cros word to thare parents. I would give the hole world if I posest it if I had never spoke a cros word to Pa nor Ma. We have had some cold nites lately. You wanted to know if I had any water melons. A comon sised [39] one heare costs a doler and every thing else in proportion. The Boys are all well in camp. You wanted to know in one of your leters how James Allen [40] was getting along. I have not sene him any the worse for whisky since we left Pontiac and I dont think he has

38. Research has not uncovered the identity of May. I suspect that she was a young lady, about Laforest's age, who either lived in the neighborhood or dated Laforest before his enlistment.

39. He means medium or average sized watermelon.

40. James Allen was a private from home—Odell Township—who was a member of Company G. James enlisted on August 5, 1862 and was discharged with the rest of the regiment on June 8, 1865.

ben. You said in your letter that Bate & John was going of to school. They must be getting up in the world. I wrote to John when we was at the Tunnel last winter and never have received an answer, and to Bate over too months ago and have not got an answer. It might be that thare getting above a soldier. You ought not wrote that Julia [41] was a going to get married it makes me fele so bad. Old spare ribs will wate till I get back I know. [42] Hoo has Dexter got on his farm this summer and how is he getting along? You cant expect much of a leter from me this time, since you wrote to me about J., so I will have to close. Love to all, C. L. Dunham.

To Mr. Simeon H. Dunham

Nashville, Tennessee, September 17, 1863

I have not much time to write much before the mail goes out but I thought I would write a few lines. I am well and harty. I just got back from Sthephenson [*sic*] [Stevenson] Alabama last nite. Thare was too trains of wonded came up to this place. Thare has been some hard fighting. We have very cold nites heare but very warm days. The boys are well. A. Ross is getting stout again. We are a going to have preaching in camp this afternoon. We drew pay a few days ago too months pay, and deductted out what we had run over our clothing. I had run over mine six dollars and twenty five cts. Some had run over thars two months pay. Delos Robinson & David Finley and Lige Schosher are a going to have each of them sent a pare of boots. If you are a mind to, you can get me a pare and send with them. We cant get a pare heare short of 12$, that is a desent pare. Dont have the upers very heavy but heavy soles, for it is so strong that it will cut a pare out in few days and a cuple pare of socks. I got Hercy's leter yesterday with that paper in it. The size of the boots I cam near forgetting number 7 are plenty large

41. Julia was a local girl engaged to a friend in Company C.
42. Some girls will not wait for their men to return from war and they marry other eligible men. Laforest is suggesting that his girl, Katie Gurnsey, who was on the slim side, would be true and wait for him. She did.

enough. The drum has just beat for meating. I will be train guard again in the morning. It takes from two to three days to make a trip. I will have to close or I wont get it in the office in time for it to go this afternoon, so I will close. Lots of love to all, C. L. Dunham.

To Mrs. Simeon H. Dunham

Nashville, Tennessee, September 22, 1863

I received yours and Hercy's leter of the 14th a day or two ago and have not had time to write since. I am well. We are on duty prety much all the time drill or some thing else. I am a going to Alabama in the morning as a guard on the cars. We will be gon two or three days. I got a leter from Eugene a day or two a go. He was well when he wrote. The boys are all well. As to sickness, A. Ross met with prety [bad] luck. He went as a guard on the train and the train stopt for them to get off. It was nite and they stopt rite over a bridg and it was so dark that he did not see the bridg and he went down through and he fell up on the hard ground. It brused him up pretty bad. It was a great wonder that it did not brake some of his bones but it did not. It smast his gun all to peaces so you can see what cind of a fall it was, but he is getting along prety well now. I dont think we will stay long at this place. We are under marching orders now. It is a poor miserable plase any how. It is a prety large city. It has ben a business plase but it is prety well shattered now. You wrote that you hurd that James Trobrge [43] was to be shot. That is all a hoax he is at Stevenson Alabama. I will probably see him tomorrow. Thare has a number of our boys seen him. I cant think of anything to write of any account and so I will close and it is getting late and I will have to get up at one or two for me to have to start out on the train at three. So I will close with lots of love, C. L. Dunham.

43. Laforest was correct; Trobridge was busted from sergeant to private but not shot and killed. Trobridge was a friend from Ottowa, Ill.; he was serving in the Illinois 104th.

TO MRS. SIMEON H. DUNHAM

Nashville, Tennessee, October 5, 1863

Once again I take a few lesure moments that I have to drop a few lines to let you know how I am a getting a long. I am well and redy for my rashens. It is a splendid morning but prety cold. I dont see but that it is just as cold down heare as it is up there. [Walter] Good just brought me in a leter from Hercy dated September 30. I tell you what it done me good to heare that you all was well. It must be very lonesome for you without H. for she said she was a going to C. P. so I supose she is thare now. Capt. Perry has not got back yet. His time was up some time a go. I expect by the time you get this leter we will be somewhare else for we are under marching orders and to be in rediness to moove at a moments warning with two days rations. We dont know yet any thing about whare we will go and we may not move for a long time. We dont know from one day to another whare we will be the next. I got a leter from Eugene some time ago and have not had time to answer it for we are on duty most all of our time. When we ant on picket we have to drill. We have company drill in the morning & Briggade drill in the afternoon. So you see that we are on the move most of our time. A. Ross has got over his fall so that he has come back to the company. D. Robinson & D. Finley are both writing. Thare is but one in our company that is sick and he has ben under the wether for a long time. We hurd heare that the news has got back thare that we was in the fight below heare,[44] but we was not. Part of our divisn was in it. The rebs got all they bargend for to. All though our boys retreated back to the entrenchments that is know sine that they was whipt back. The rebs charged on our boys seven times a day or too ago and was repulsed evry time. Our boys wer in the entrenchments. The rebs charged eight deep. They said our boys

---

44. All references to fighting "below heare" concerns the massive military operations around Chattanooga. The battle had long since been joined and the heroics, casualties, and importance of the operation were being observed by the whole nation.

just mowed them down. I dont know of any more news to write so I will close with lots of love so good by, C. L. Dunham.

To Mr. Simeon H. Dunham

Nashville, Tennessee, October 11, 1863

I am on duty today so I take this present opportunity to drop you a few lines to let you know that I am well. We just got back from Columbus [*sic*] [Columbia] last nite. We had just got to bed Wednesday nite and the order came for ous to get up and have three days rations in our haversacks and be ready to march so about nine o' clock we found ourselves on the cars bound for Columbus [Columbia] in this state. When we got within eight miles of thare, we got of the cars and marched in to town about one o' clock in the afternoon. They was expecting an attack rate a way. We stayd thare last night and the order came the next morning for to march back to Franklin that is 28 miles. So we started at eleven o' clock and we got thare about noon the next day (yesterday). Half of the regiment stayd at F. [ranklin] When we went down we took the cars thare and feched up home again, as we cold [*sic*] [called] it, all safe and sound. The rebs have got columbus [Columbia] now. Thare was not but a part of a regiment of our men thare and thare was to many rebs coming on to them, so thay had to leve the place, but they wont stay thare long. They got one good flaxing before they got thare. If we had our hole regiment thare we would stood them a fight. Thare was four thousand strong of the rebs, all cavelry. I don't see what our men wanted to keep troops thare for, for thare ant any thing thare. I gues that will be enough of that. The bels are ringing for church down in the city. We are campt rite in the eye of the city. The regiment has all drawn ruber blankets so you nede not send me any. The boys are all well and redy for a fight if it is needed, but I dont think we will get in to one very soon. Thare is a going to be a bluds [45] (down at the front) before long, if the rebs

45. The reference is to blood, or rather a bloody battle in the offing.

stand. I think if we whip them out thare the war will sone come to close. We are a getting a heavy force thare and so are the rebs. They know it is life or death thare. They know if they are whipt thare they are gon up salt crick. It beats all how they stick to it so when thare is so many disserting them. I cant think of anything more to write that amounts to anything so I will close with lots of love to you all, C. L. Dunham.

To Miss Hercey Dunham

Nashville, Tennessee, October 20, 1863

I received your leter several days ago but have not had time to answer it untill now. I have not ben in camp more than too days for more than a weak. I was off on train guard. We dont get time to do our washing let alone anything else. When we are not on picket or guard of some kind we are on drill. We have company drill and Battallian in the morning & Briggade in the afternoon but let them saill in. It is all in a fellows life time. Our time will soon be half up.[46] I wish you could just step in and see how we have got our tent aranged. We have got a stove in it and bunks for beads and a plenty to eat so you see we are all OK. I got a leter from home yesterday. They wer all well when they wrote. I am a going down to the exspress office this afternoon to see if thare aint some thing thare for me from home. I sent fore somethings and they sent them the 14th, so if they came rite through they are heare by this time. Diner is ready so I will have to go and eat or I wont get any for it is evry one for himself heare. I have eaten my diner so I will let you know what we had for diner. We had boild beaf, stude beans, bakers bread & coffee, and I had some butter on my bread to. D. Robinson's mother sent him some & he gave me some to putt on my bread. I tell you what is went tip top. We will have to go out on Battalion drill at half past one o clock. It looks as iff it was a going to rain. It has raind the most of the time for too weaks. The hole of

46. Laforest's enlistment was just about one-half completed.

the regiment has drawn ruber blankets. It must be awful lonesome
for Ma now since you left. I hope the war will sone be over so that
I can be at home once more but it looks dark. I will have to close
for I will have to go out on drill son. Give my respects to Mr. & Mrs.
Coffin and the rest of the folks so I will close with these few lines
hopeing they will find you well. Tell Eugene that he must take
good care of himself. I would have writen some to him but I have
not time so I will close with lots of love to yourself & Eugene, good
by for this time, C. L. Dunham.

To Mr. and Mrs. Simeon H. Dunham

Nashville, Tennessee, October 28 and 30, 1863

I take these few lesure moment to answer your leter to let you
know that I am well and that I got my boots. I just got back last
nite from the front; the hole company went. We was gon just a
weak. We came back to Nashville with the forth engine. Three of
them got broke and the rebels placed a torpedo under the track and
blew the engine up, but it did not hurt any one. It roared like a
cannon that delaid ous one day so we went out in the mountains a
huntain. Thare was lots of squrls and wild turkeys. That was about
all the gaim we could find but thare is a plenty of rebs thare. The
railroad runs rite through the mountains. The tunnel is a mile long
& takes too or three engines to pull a train up through the mountains. My boots are just the thing & stockings to. They will last as
long as eight pare of the stockings that we get heare. That candy is
tip top. The boys are all well. I got a leter last eavning from
E. Earp & Jane. They wer all well when they wrote. I got one from
Hercy to the same time so that made three all at once.

Oct. th 30. I had to stop writing and eat my dinner the other day &
after we got done we had to write out on drill & the next morning
we went on picket so I didnt get a chance to write untill now. I
should have writen that night out [but] we had know candels. I
have just got off of picket. Iff you had seene me last night between
12 and 2 o clock you would have seene me walking my beat as

chearful as a mouse but my mind was on home. It raind pretty much all night, my boots went tip top. I expect I will go on train guard again in the morning or tomorrow night. I wodent wonder if we would stay heare this winter. We have got a splendid camp. We dont heare any more about furlow but I guess they will get to giveing them before long. The troops are haveing a hard time down to the front. They are liveing on half or less rations. They have so much bother on the railroad that they cant get rations to them fast enough. They wer fighting thare the first of the weak when we was down thare. I dont think of anything more to write now so I will close with lots of love and hopeing these few lines will find you all well, C. L. Dunham.

To Mrs. Simeon H. Dunham

Nashville, Tennessee, November 8, 1863

I received your leter a day or too ago but I have not had time to answer it till now. We had Regimental inspection this morning just got through. Your leter found me well & harty. I tell you what was I was glad to heare that you are all well. As long as I can heare from home and hear that you are all well then I am all rite. I just came off of train guard last eavening. We had a pleasant trip. I got a leter from H. two or three days ago. I expect she will be home before you get this would that I could go home when I pleas. If I could you mite be ashurd that I would be thare this morning but that litle word if is in the way. I can see you all thare at home the same as it use to be sunday or it seems so, but it cant be as it use to be. You may think strange sometimes that I dont write any more but when I look back and see how things have changed for a year back and get to thinking of home I cant write. It is a splendid morning some what cool. We have not had any snow heare yet but it has ben cold enough for it. We have a cold rain about evry too or three days. The Regiment is very healthey that is not any of the boys in the company sick so as to be in the hospital. The bells are ringing in town for meating but we cant go without a pass from the Colonel. Ante that rough, but that is milatory as the hous call it. We expect to get paid off this weak. We send the pay roals las night. Our troops have drove the rebs back so that our boats are runing up the tenisee river up to chattanooga and the railroad to. For my part I dont see how the rebs are a going to stand it this winter. I know if our army was as bad off as they are they could not keep me five minutes, but thank fortune we have plenty to eat and ware butt I have seen the time when I jump at a crumb but that is all in a persons lifetime. It is sunday but if you was heare I dont believe you would think it was sunday for the fidles and other kinds of music are ratteling away, some singing some a little of everything. I believe I have writen all that amounts to anything so I will close with lots of love to all, C. L. Dunham.

To All the Family at Home

Nashville, Tennessee, November 12, 1863

Once more I improve the time in writing to you to let you know that I am well and harty. We have none drill this morning but all the boys are out of the tent but one and he is writing so it is as still as a church mouse but it ant often the case. I got Mas leter of the 5th yesterday. Do you get any of the papers that I have sent? I have sent a number. I sent one yesterday to Hiram. We are looking for to be paid off every day, but we are not shure of it till we get it in our hands. We are haveing splendid wether pretty cool but we have not had any snow yet. I dont know whether I ever wrote to you anything about what kind of a looking place it is heare. The sity has been quite a nice place for the South. Our campes on the east side of the city about a mile of[f] the river are clost to Fort Negly.[47] Thare is thre forts heare all in a row about a mile a part. First is Fort Negly, Fort Defiance and Fort Confiscation. The last covers 14 acres of ground and thare is 15 seige guns planted around the city. One of them is right in one camp, it carries a 120 pound

47. Fort Negley.

shell. The news was good last eavening if it is only true. The news was that the rebs got a good thrashing and that our troops had taken Ten thousand prisinors.[48] For my part I dont believe that the war will last longer than spring but we cant tell but time will tell. We dont have so much duty to do as we have [had]. Thare has some more troops came heare. Ma, you said in your last leter that you tride to get hiram to write. I expect that he thinks so much of them wegen gals that he dont ever think of me. But just wate till I get back, I will throw him down to pay for it. I dont think of anything more so I will close, lots of love, C. L. Dunham.

TO MR. SIMEON H. DUNHAM

Nashville, Tennessee, November 17, 1863

I have not much time to write for it is bed time now and I have got to go on the train at three o clock in the morning, but thought a few words would be beter than non for I may not get a chance to write again for a weak. I am well and harty. We got our pay this eavening. I will send you five dollars in this leter and I will send more as I write along. Has any one taken up that land that Palmer gave up? If it is unocipide let me know in your next leter and find out whether a person can let the county have the hundred dollars and take forty acres of land. One of the boys in the company would like to do that way if he could. I said boy but he is a married man. We are all boys heare. He is a tip top fellow. We had Briggade inspection today. Day after tomorrow we have grand review but I wont be heare, I tell you what I am glad of it too. I got a leter from Hurcy yesterday. I am glad that she has got home again for I know that it must have ben lonesome while she was gon. I will have to bring my leter to a close for I have got to fry a lot of meat to take along and fix my bread in my haversack and grind my coffee so I wont have much time. I should have writen today but we have ben on the go all day so you must not think hard because I

48. He is discussing victories at Chattanooga.

dont wright more. So good by for this time. Lots of love to all, C. L. Dunham.

To Miss Hercey Dunham

Nashville, Tennessee, November 21, 1863

I have not much news to write but I thought I would wright a few lines as I have nothing to do this morning. I am well and able for my rations. It raind all day yesterday and it is awful mudy this morning. One of the boys in the company died day before yester-day. He got in to a row and got stabd so that he died in two days after. He was a tip top solder only he would get on a spree once in a while. I got a leter from John S. a day or two ago. I have got too from him within three weeks and I got one from B[atie]. The mail just came in. I thought shure I would get one from some of you thare at home but I was disappointed. I wrote a leter to Pa. too or three days ago and put five dollars in it. I shal put five or tenn in this. I am most afraid to put tenn in for fear it wont go. You said that J.[ane] wanted to know if I fell out of bed lately. I have not fell out but I have got jurked out. We have great times pulling one another out of bead but if I did fall out I would not have far to fall. I expect I will be on train guard tomorrow morning. We had a tip top time the last time I was down. We was gon two days. The leter that I wrote to Pa I wrot in the eavening before we started. I think shure will be another fight soon down at the front, if the rebs stand. Things look prety favorable on our side now I believe. I have writen all that amounts to anything so I will come to a close so good by lots of love to all. I will send tenn dollars, C. L. Dunham.

To Mrs. Simeon H. Dunham

Nashville, Tennessee, December 9, 1863

I received your leter just a few minutes ago dated the third. I was a going to wright as soon as I eat my breakfast this morning but some thing seme to tell me to wait [for] I was a going to get a leter from home. So I did wait and shure enough I did get one. I am well and harty as ever excepting a bad coald but that aint much for a solder. I got in last night off of the cars about seven o clock. I was gon two days. We had a fine time on our train but the train just ahead of ous had an awful smash up, but it hapend not to kill any one. The boys of my company was on it. We go by companys, a Co. for two trains. We brought back a lot of rebs, about four hundred I should think. The most of them say they are willing to stop fighting and go home. I should think they would for such a looking set I never saw before, know close scarcely nor shoes on thare feat. I tell you what it is pretty cold down heare. I got a leter from Eugene last eavning. He was well when he wrote. I got Ephram Earps leter three or four days ago. It is curious whi Jane dont get my leters. She said in E. letter that she had not got one from me since last spring and I know that I have writen several. I wrote one to her not but two or three days after I wrote to Ephram. When you send that Christmas diner send me some fride cakes. You know how I use to make them git. I got the butter and cheas that you sent. I tell you what it goes tip top, that is what makes a solder grin. You said in one of your leters that you hurd that we was liveing on half rations. We did for a while when they had such a hard time getting rations down to the front but then we got a long first rate. You must not believe every thing that you heare about ous for you heare I know three times more than is true. You wanted to know if I took that paper that I sent to H. I get one from our chaplin evry sunday and sometime it is that kind and some times some other. When you send that Christmas diner I would like it if Pa would send me some of that medicin that he gave me when I left home, some of them powders. I dont think of any thing more so I will bring my leter to a close with lots of love to all, C. L. Dunham.

To Miss Hercey Dunham

Nashville, Tennessee, December 13, 1863

I have know news to write but I thought I would drop you a few lines. I should have writen this morning but I thought I would wait untill tomorrow and I might get a leter from some of you, but come to find out I have got to go on the train at three o clock in the morning so I might not get a chance to wright untill the last of the weak. I am well as usual. It has raind prety mutch all the time for three or four days not very cold. I got a leter from Eugene not but a few days ago. They was well when he wrote. I have not seen Chester since I staid all night with him but I shal try and see him tomorrow. Have you got my letter that I told about my seeing him? You had beter wright to him for I should judge that he was considerably down harted, but if you do wright to him dont say anything about that I said he was down harted for he told me to tell you that he felt as well as ever. Litle did I think that a leter would do me so mutch good as it does before I left home. I gess I did not wright in any of my leters about my comeing a crost the E. P.[49] boys. I saw fore or five of the boys. They are stationd at the siege guns heare. They said that they saw you when you was out thare to EP. They had just come from Le . . .[50] when I first saw them. I have ben amuseeing myself today by reading my old leters from home. We dont have anything scarcley to read heare so that time passes so slow when we are in camp. We have past the resulations that we will go to bead that is in my tent. The boys are all tip top boys in my tent. I dont think of anything more to wright, so I will bring my leter to a close with lots of love to all, C. L. Dunham.

To Mr. Hiram Dunham

Nashville, Tennessee, December 17, 1863

I just received your and Pa and Mas leter this morning. I am glad to heare that you are all well. Your leter found me well and harty as a buck. It beats all why you dont get my leters. I know that I have writen once and twice a weak. I have not much news to write but a litle may be beter than non. I just got back off of the train last eavening. We had a very good trip on our train but the train just behind ous run off and kild three of our soldiers and hurt

49. E. P. is an abbreviation for Eppards Point Township in Livingston County, Illinois.

50. It is impossible to determine the exact spelling of this word.

several others prety bad. I tell you what thare is a good many ways of killing people down heare. The train guard is stopt now and I am glad of it. You spoke of enlisting in your leter. If you know what is good for yourself you will stay at home and help Pa and Ma all you can. I tell you what but you may think it is not so. You would not stand it six months. By the time you had ben through what I have, you would sing a diferent song and say give me home. You would say, or iff you did not say it you would think it, O if I was at home in my Pas house and in a good bed that my dear mother made how nice it would be. But then it would be to late. For my part I have wished it a good many times. You dont know what it is too lay out all night in the cold rain and have to get up evry morning at just such a time cold or rainy makes know diference. If you ar detailed you have got to go rane or shine. You said in your leter that it was the same old thing over and over thare. I would like to know what you would call it heare. You would sooner wish yourself in prison than to be bound so. Cant go anywhare with out a pass and we have got to do just so whether we wan to or not. What do you think of that Hiram? If you think anything of me stay at home. We have lost one dear Brother in this war and may be I wont get out of it yet alive. But as for myself I am willing to stand it but I dont want any more brothers in this war if it can be helpt. Hiram stay at home and be a good boy and when I get back we will have a good time. I dont think of anything more to write so I will close with lots of love to all . . . I would fill this side to some of you but we have run out of wood and it is so cold that I can hardly wright. Thare is five dollars yet that pa has not got yet unless he has got it since he wrote for I sent twenty dollars. Know more at present so good by, C. L. Dunham.

To Mr. and Mrs. Simeon H. Dunham

Nashville, Tennessee, December 22, 1863

I take this present opportunity to drop you a few lines to let you know that I am well. We are haveing splendid weather heare now. I have not got a leter from any of you for more than a weak but I guess I will get one tomorrow. I would put off wrighting untill tomorrow and see if I did not get one but I will be on picket. We have had some very cold nights long back for standing picket. We dont have to go on train guard any more so I wont get to see weather any more. I expect you are having prety cold weather thare now. I wich I could be thare but that is all the good it does. I think they will get to giveing furlows again soon. We dont have so much duty to do as we have had. Thare is talk about our going back to Gallitan but I cant see it in that light but I hope we will. Our Colonel is thare now. Dinner is most ready and then I will make army rations. The drum is beating for roll call so I will have to stop a few minutes. I have got don eating my diner. After rool call was over dinner was ready. We have Battalion drill this after-noon; had company drill this morning. They ar bound that we shall be drild right up to the handel. Our Regiment is sead to be one of the best drild in the service. We hav taken the rug of the bush evry time on grand review. We have had three grand reviews within a month. It is a splendid sight to see so many Regiments a moveing. The boys are all well in our company. Christmas is prety close at hand. Would that I could be thare to eat a Christmas dinner. It aint the diner that I would care for but to see my dear Mother and the rest of the loved ones at home. Dont wory about me. If it should be that we will never meat again in this world I hope we will in another. I dont think of any more to write so I will close with lots of love to all, C. L. Dunham

To Mrs. Simeon H. Dunham

Nashville, Tennessee, December 27, 1863

I received your leter of the 20th yesterday. I tell you what I was glad to heare that you was all well. Your leter found me harty as usual. It is raining heare a little this morning but it is prety warm. We was to have Briggade inspection this morning but the rain stopt ous so we will have it tomorrow, but I guse I will be on picket. You spoke about it being so cold and blustering in your leter of the 15th and how bad you felt for fear that I was on picket and it would be so cold. We have not had any very bad weather heare yet this winter for picketing. Yet we have had some prety cold nights but it has ben dry. It is beter a cold nit than it is when it rains. I dont mind picket that goes off first trate. We had a joly time heare Christmas. We took a wagen and put an long rope in the end of the tung and a lot of ous got hold of it and drew it up to the Colonels tent and we made him get in but he was very willing to and then we put four or five more officers in and then we went down town a biteing and we drew up to a brewery and then we made them treat to the bear [*sic*] [beer] and then they got in again and then we went for camp and when we got thare the Colonel give ous a speache. We are going to give some of the rest of the officers a round New Years. It beats all why you dont get my leters. I have writen one evry weak and sometimes two and I sent 20$, five in one, teen in another, and five in another. I wouldnt wonder if Peters sister got the leter and kept it for it was about that time you said you sent by him. The boys are all well in my co. They thought one had the small pox but it was not, he was just a litle unwell. Thare wasent but one in the regiment that has got it, but thare is good many cases in the city. They are calling for diner so I will stop writeing for a few minutes.

Now I have got dun with my dinner so I will try it again. First place I will let you know what I had for dinner. Wal I had boild beef, bakers bread, honey, apple buter, plum buter, and butter and coffee. So you see I had a wolf meal. My partner or the fellow that bunks with me had thoes things sent from home. His name is Henry Hallam. He use to go to school . . . [with] A. We have three cooks one white man and too Niggers. The white mans name is James McClure. I saw Chester a day or to after I received your leter stateeing that he was down heare.[51] I stayd one nite and one day with him. I tell you what he was surprised to see me. He did not know me at first. We had a good time together. I have not seen

51. Chester was a young man from home and a good friend of the Dunham family. In fact, he was Hercey's boy friend.

him since. We dont go on train guard any more so it aint likely that
I will see him very soon again. I dont think of any more too write
so I will close with lots of love to all and a good lot for yourself.
. . . Do you know hoo sent Frank Barr [52] that can of butter in that
box of mine? He dont know and he wanted one to find out, C. L.
Dunham

To Mrs. Simeon H. Dunham

Nashville, Tennessee, January 10, 1864

I have not mutch news to write but a litle may be beter than
non. I received yours and H. leter dated the 8 of last month New
Years morning. I hope you all had a good time New Years. We had
a very good time heare. We did not get the box that you sent untill
too or three days ago, evey thing was all right. I tell you what them
fried cakes tasted like home. The turkey was tip top. It is very cold
heare but we keep as warm as we can in our tents, but it is awful to
see how many women and children ar suffering in this city. Wood
is $60 a cord. One woman that lives right heare by our camp frose
her feat so that they will have to be cut off. The boys are all well
and harty in our company. I have not got a leter from Eugene for a
good while. I dont think he got my last leter. I shall write to him
again in a day or too. I will be on picket in the morning. The drum
is beatting for roal call so I will have to stop a few minutes.

After roll call. I stayd [*sic*] [stowed] some more of uncle
Sams rations. I just eat the last of the cakes for dinner. Those papers
that you sent are first trate. I wish I had some more of them. I have
read them through and through. When we get paid off again I gues
one of the boys and myself will send and take the *Cristian Advocate*.
I am a going to meatting down in the city tonite, if I aint cald on for
duty. A person never knows for surtain when he is wanted heare. It
is thawing some today but not enough to amount to mutch. The

52. The young man mentioned here is Private Benjamin F. Barr of Company
C. He also hailed from Esmen Township. He enlisted on August 12, 1862 and
was discharged on June 8, 1865.

people heare say that they have not seen it as cold heare for a good many years. I cant think of any more to write. In fact I cant think of anything to day. One reson is that I have ben laying around camp for three or four days and I have got so uneasy that I can hardly sit still. I will close and try to do beter the next time. Lots of love to all and a right smart for yourself, C. L. Dunham.

To Mr. Simeon H. Dunham   *135426*

Nashville, Tennessee, January 17, 1864

I received yours and mas leter of the third yesterday. I am glad to heare that you ar all well. Your letter found me well and harty. I have not mutch news to write but I will do the best I can. It has ben very cold heare not mutch snow but evry thing was coverd with ice. We had to keep big fiers on the picket line to keep warm. I did not suffer any only I did not sleep mutch of any for four or five nites. Thare was 5 soldiers frose to death on the train comeing from Chattanooga to this place. The citizens suffered awfully heare. Wood was as high as $60 a cord. It has ben quite warm for three or four days. The rain is just comeing right down now. Jim Hase [53] got heare day before yesterday. He has got the mumps. He thinks he had a hard time a comeing through but he dont know anything about it yet. The boys are all well that your acquainted with. I got that box all safe. The stuffing in the turkey was tip top. I wrote you a leter some time ago stateing that I had got it. I presume you have got it by this time. Ma said that she sent a leter Monday before the one of the third. I have not got it yet. Now a little about the war. For my part I dont think it is a going to wind up very soon. The eastern army has got to have a good thrashing before thare will be mutch change but we cant tell mutch about it. The rebs are agoing to hold out as long as they can but let them slide. They will get enough of southern rights after a while. I would like to come back thare and clean out the copperheads. I

53. James A. Hayes was a new recruit from Pontiac. He enlisted on December 17, 1863 and was later transferred to Company I of the 16th Illinois Infantry.

will bet some of them will wish that they never had seen day light iff we ever got back thare. Shooting is too good for them. We will teach them how we turne the rebs down heare. I dont think of anything more to write so I will come to a close with lots of love to all you all, C. L. Dunham.

To Mrs. Simeon H. Dunham

Nashville, Tennessee, January 26, 1864

I received your letter of the 11th last Friday. I was on picket and one of the boys brought it out too me. It found me well and harty. I am glad to heare that you ar all well. As long as I can heare from home and heare that you ar all well then I am all right. I should have ritten sooner but Saturday morning I came off of picket and in the afternoon we had Regimental inspection, Sunday I did not feel like writeing and monday (yesterday) I was wood chopper. We had a good time out in the country. We went out some six or seven miles. I tell you what we make the rebs would git.[54] The road was compleatly lind with government teams loaded with wood. We are haveing splendid weather heare now. It makes me feal as if I ought to be at home too work but that cant be. I am sory to heare that Jane is sick. The boys are all well in my company that you are acquainted with. We had preaching in camp sunday. Thare was several ladies present, Lieutenant Culvers wife and seven others. I got a leter from Eugene a day or too ago. He was well when he wrote. I dont think we will stay heare mutch longer but we cant tell for surtain. When we do leave heare it aint likely that we will get letters through so often. If you dont you must not wory about me for it wont make it a bit better. I have found since I have ben in this show that a person mite as well take things as it comes. I will be on picket tomorrow. We have good times on picket now. We have four reliefs so that we only have six ours of twenty four to stand. Thare is several a going out of our

54. Confederate prisoners were made to gather wood for the Union forces.

Regiment to Ill.[inois] for recruits. I dont know whether any one will go out of our company or not. I expect we will have drill this afternoon. The boys are haveing great times this pleasant weather playing marbels and one thing and another. I dont think of anything more to write so I will come to a close with lots of love to all and a rite smart change for yourself, C. L. Dunham.

To Mrs. Sarah Jane Dunham

Nashville, Tennessee, January 28, 1864

I take this present opportunity to drop you a few lines to let you know that I am well. I got a letter from home this morning stateing that you was sick. I am sory to hear that you ar sick. I hope you will get well. We ar haveing splendid wether heare now. In my letter from home this morning Pa said that you had not got a letter from me yet. You must not feal hard of me becos you have not received any from me. I have written time after time and shal continue to do so. I think it was the last letter that I wrote to you directed it in care of Ephram.[55] We ar a going to leave heare in a few days and like enough before nite. We have marching orders now. As near as I can find out whare we ar a going is that we ar a going too Chattanoga. That will be about 150 miles that we have got to march. I think it is a shame that they dont take ous on the cars, but know. We have all ways had to take it on foot and will have to keep going so till our time is out. I will have to stop writeing a few minutes to eat my dinner.

Now I have got my dinner eat so I will try it once more. The health of the Regiment as a general thing is very good. Thare is a few caces of the small pox, but it dont seme to be spreding mutch. We had a very good time heare Christmas and New Years all though it was very cold. I was on picket last nite was relieved this morning and as soon as I got into camp I had to go to washing and mending and getting ready for our journey. I will have to close for

---

55. Ephram Earp was Jane's brother.

it is time that I had the leter in the office so I close with lots of love. I will direct it to Ephram, you will be more apt to get it, C. L. Dunham.

To Mrs. Simeon H. Dunham

Nashville, Tennessee, January 30, 1864

I received yours and H.'s letter of the 16th a day or to ago. I am glad to heare that you are all well. I am well and harty. I have not mutch time to write for we are so buisy getting ready for to march. We take up the line of march tomorrow morning. I expect we are a going to Chattanooga. We will have it to march. It is about 150 miles. I dont know when I will get a chance to write again but I will write as soon as I can get a chance. You will write as usual. I will get the letters. That cake was splendid—too good for a soldier. The boys ar all well. I must stop writeing for we have got to draw purp tents as we call them. They ar little tents big enough a for too. You must not feal hard becas I dont write anymore this time for I would write more if I had time. So I close with lots of love to all and a good lot for yourself, C. L. Dunham.

To Mr. Simeon H. Dunham

Nashville, Tennessee, February 4, 1864

I received your and Hurcyes letter of the 24 of last month yesterday. It found me well. I am sory to heare that Ma is sick. I hope she will not be very sick. Would that I could heare this morning how she is but that cant be. Our camp is all tore up. We expected to leave heare several days ago but the Generals got into a mus [*sic*] [fuss] among themselves, so I gues we wont leave heare for some time. We was a going to the front thate is too Briggades heare. I gues the other Briggade will go in our place. If they do we wont leave hear this summer. We have not received the last box you sent yet. The boys are all well. A. Ross has gon in the invalid corps or rather put in. He has not got over that fall that he got last summer. You said in yore letter that you thought the war would not last six months longer. I think we will be home by fall. I dont see how the rebs can stand it mutch longer. Since the last battle down heare thare has eight thousand rebles disserters came in and give them selves up. We ar haveing splendid wether heare now, rather cool but pleasant. Has Jane got the money that was comeing to A. yet? Colonel Cropsey is at home on a furlow. I expect you have seen him by this time. I dont think of anything more to writ. In fact we dont have any newes to write. Hopeing these few lines will find you all well. I will close with lots of love to all. I wrote this with a lead pensel for evry thing is tore up so that I had now place to write, C. L. Dunham.

To Miss Hercey Dunham

Nashville, Tennessee, February 12, 1864

I have not mutch to write but a little may be beter than non. I am well and harty. I received your leter of the 30th several days ago but I have not had time to write. We have ben so buisy a building houses and fixing our camp that we tore up so when we was a going to leave but we have got in good shape again now. I received yours and Mas leter of the 3d yesterday. You cant think how glad I was to see that Ma had written some and to know that she was getting well. It takes a great weight off of my mind. We are haveing splendid weather heare all most like summer. I got a letter from Ephram Earp yesterday. He did not say how Jane was. A. Ross is pretty sick, they took him off to the hospital this morning. He had the mumps in the first place. He is haveing rather bad luck. All the rest of the boys ar well. I got a letter from Batie several days ago. I got that photograph of Eugene that you sent me. E. wanted me to send him mine so I went down town yesterday and got it taken. I could not get one unless I took a half dozen. I dont get them untill tomorrow so when I write again I will send one home. I got the last box that Pa and Ma sent on the 5th. The cakes wer moldy but the aples wer all rite, the losengers were nice. We have drill evry day now. We will have Briggade drill this afternoon. I presume we will stay heare some time like enough all summer. You wanted to know the boys names that ar in my mess. You dont know any of them but I will give you thare names: James Reuston, Clinton Guise, Peter Shaphel, and my bead fellows name is David Harbinson.[56] He lives neare to Dwight when he is at home. The three first ar married men. Thare use to be more in our mess but when we tore up for to leave heare we drawd small tents. I dont think of any thing more to write so I will close with lots of love to all. I will write to ma in a few days. I will express Pa 14$ some time next weak, C. L. Dunham.

To Mrs. Simeon H. Dunham

Nashville, Tennessee, February 17, 1864

We are still at N. and know prospect of leaveing very soon. I am well as usual. We ar haveing splendid wether heare now but rather cool. People are plowing. It makes me feal as if I ought to be at home to work but that is out of the question. Ma, pen cant discribe how glad I was to see you had written some in Hurceys last letter that I received and to know that you was getting well. As long as things are right at home I can stand it heare and things go off smooth. I got a letter from E. Earp a day or too ago. It has ben some time since I got a letter from Eugene. A. Ross is still at the hospital but he is some better. I believe the rest of the boys ar all well. Thare is know more cases of the small pox in our Regt. I said in my last letter that I wrot to H. that I would express Pa some

56. James Ruston was a private from Livingston County. He enlisted on August 11, 1862 and was discharged as a corporal on June 8, 1865. Clinton Guise was also a Company C boy who hailed from Livingston County. He enlisted and was discharged the same day as Ruston. Private Peter P. Sharer was from Amity Township. Peter enlisted on August 13, 1862 and was discharged on May 23, 1864. David Harbeson hailed from Livingston County. He enlisted on August 9, 1862, rose to the rank of corporal, and was discharged with most of the rest of the Regiment on June 8, 1865.

money, but I wont send it rite away unless Pa neads it. If he does, write and I will send it. I was down through the city this morning. I went down to get my photographs that I had taken but they was not doen. I will get them this eavening so when I write again I will send one. We have Battalion drill this afternoon. The drums ar a beating for noon roal call so I will stop writeing till after dinner.

Now I have eaten my dinner so I will try to write a little more. First place I will let you know what I had for dinner. We had Bakers Bread, Boild Beaf and Coffee. One thing I came nere forgetting, I had some Butter to. Some that one of the boys had sent from home. I dont think of anything more to writ that will amount to anything so I will close with lots of love to all and a good lot for yourself, C. L. Dunham.

To Mrs. Simeon H. Dunham

Nashville, Tennessee, February 23, 1864

I take a few lesure moments that I have this morning to drop you a few lines to let you know that I am well. It is most a splendid spring morning heare this morning. I received Pas, Her. and your letter of the 12th yesterday. Now you can see how the letters come through that was tenn days a coming through. I know by the way you write that you dont begin to get all the letters that I write, for I write evry weak and often twice a weak. I got a letter from Eugene yesterday. It was 12 days a comeing through. We had annother tare up [57] yesterday to leave but I dont think we will very soon. Thare semes to be considerable trouble amonxt the Generals. One said that our Briggade shall go and one sais we shant. You se thare is too Briggades neare and they bothe wan to get away from heare. So it is hard telling whitch will leave. Thare is not any more in our Regiment that has got the small pox. Thare was only three or four that had it. I wrote you a leter some time ago stateing that I had received the last box. You have got it [my letter] by this time, I presume. I got that medicine all right. I got them stamps that you

57. The brigade dismantled all tents and prepared to move out to the south.

spoke of in your letter. Thare was some in the one that I got yesterday. I got the paper four or five days before I got the letter. If we stay heare I gues I will get a furlow in the spring or summer sometime. They have commensed giveing them again. I put in for one but they are a going to let the married men go first. Delos Robinson has got one maid out and it is sent to the front to be sind. You see they have to [be] sind by Genl. Grant but I would not say anything about it to his folks for he may not get it. The boys are all well. I have not seen Chester since that time that I stayed all nite with him. I gues I will write to him today. I dont think of anything more to write of any account so I will come to a close. Lots of love to all. You must recollect that when I write to one it is for all. Hiram, I wan to heare from you once in a while. If I dont I will take you throough a corse of sprants [*sic*] [sprints] when I get back so you had better look out, C. L. Dunham

To Mrs. Simeon H. Dunham

Unidentified camp on the road south, February 27, 1864

You will se by this that I have left N. We have ben on the march four days. We have had a good time for marching so far. I dont know whare we ar bound. I am as harty as ever. I received your letter on the 19th this morning at Murfreesboro. We campt thare last nite. It was rather dusty getting a long today. We marched 14 miles today. I dont feal mutch like writeing and I would not to any other place but home. I am lying flat on the ground or rather on my blankets in my purp tent so you can see that I have not got a very good place to write. We ar within 11 miles of Shelbyville, Tenn. I dont know whether this will go or not but I gues they will leave the mail thare. We will get thare by tomorrow noon. We take up the line of march evry morning by day light & the boys are all rite and lively. I dont think of anything more to write so I will close with lots of love to all and a good lot for yourself. Direct your letters the same as ever to N. [ashville] I will write as often as I can, C. L. Dunham.

To Mr. Simeon H. Dunham

In an Alabama campsite for the night, March 6, 1864 [58]

I thought I would drop you a few lines to let you know that I am alive and well all though I dont feal mutch like writeing. We have been marching all day so you can immagin how I feal. We have had very mudy hard roads for several days. We just got over the mountains last night. We was on the mountains most of too days. When we get through I will give you a discription of our march. The Boys ar all well. I stopt writeing for a few minutes to draw my rations for tomorrow. We will be on the other side of the Tenn. River if nothing happens tomorrow. I dont think of anything more to write at present so I will come to a close. You must not think hard of me becase I dont write any more for I feal more like takeing a nap than writeing, so I close with lots of love to all, C. L. Dunham.

To Mr. and Mrs. Simeon H. Dunham and Family

Chattanooga, Tennessee, March 13, 1864

I take this present opportunity to drop you a few lines to let you know that I am alive and well. We have got to our journeys end for the present. We got heare on the 11th; we left Nashville on the 24th of last month. We marched something like 170 miles but it is only 150 by the railroad. We ar in camp six miles from Chattanogga in Lookout valley right at the foot of Lookout Mountain, right whare our boys charged up when they took it. I tell you what it is a grand sight. The mountain is something like one mile and a half high. We had very hard marching the last weak. It was so wet and muddy and the last day was very hot. We have ben in too

---

58. At the time Laforest wrote this letter he was just north and a little west of Bridgeport, Alabama, just south of the Tennessee state line. He and his brigade would then march east and touch the northwestern corner of Georgia on their way to Chattanooga.

states besides Tenn. since we left N.—Alabama & Georgia. We are
with in one mile and a half of the Georgia line now. I tell you what
we had a ruff old time a comeing over the mountains out of our
train. Thare was thirty or forty mules died so you can guess
what kind of a time we had, and thare is know telling how many
wageons smashed down. For my part I dont see how the rebs ever
maid a liveing down heare for it is nothing but rocks and mountains. Know wonder that they wanted war so that they could get
something to eat. Let people talk about thare balm of a thousand
flowers but we can beat that heare, we have the balm of a thousand
mules. The roads ar strewd with dead mules. It beats any thing I
ever hurd tell of. If I could see you I could tell you of my great
sights but it would take me a month of sundays to wright it. I
received mas & Hercys letter of the 5th this morning. I am glad to
heare that you ar all well. Time slides off fast when I heare from
home often and heare that you are all well. I got H. & Janes letter
yesterday. I received Pas & Mas & Hercys letter of the 27th of last
month when we was at BridgePort. I tell you what that was the
kind of a letter I like, a regular family letter. I have not had time to
answer it untill now for we have ben on the move all the time. I got
the stamps you spoke about. I saw one of the boys out of Chesters
Reg a few days ago and he said he was well. The boys are all well.
Our first leiutenant is at BridgePort sick with the small pox but he
has it very light. I will send you annother photograph of mine. You
will see thare is a speak [*sic*] [speck] under the left eye. I dont
know what maid it. I did not wan to take them but I thought I had
better for I would not get another chance to get them taken. I dont
think of anything more so I will close with lots of love, C. L. Dunham

To Mr. Simeon H. Dunham

Lookout Mountain, Tennessee, March 20, 1864

I received yours & Mas letter of the 27 yesterday. It found me
well and harty. I am glad to heare that you ar all well and getting

along well. We have got settled down again but dont know how long we will stay, so we have got tip top houses maid. Four in a house. We ar haveing splendid wether but rather coal. Snowed a litle yesterday. We had grand review yesterday by Gen. Howard [59] and Gen. Hooker.[60] The way they ar fixing up it looks as if we was a going to stay heare all summer but thare is know telling how long we will stay. Our camp is right in the woods. It suits me & must as well if not a litle better than it did in N.[ashville] and I know it will be better for a good many in the Reg. We will go on duty once in about twenty days. So you see we will have a good thing of it if we stay heare but thare is that little word if. I exspect we will get paid off soon and if we do I will send thirty five or forty dollars. I would have sent some last pay day but thare was some hopes of my getting a furlow but they will isue an order one day to give furlows and the next day countermand it. That is the way things go in this show but let them pitch in, it is all in a persons lifetime. You spoke about the surplus rations or company funds when we was at N. It amounted to something like one hundred and sixty dollars but we dont get the money but the Captain bies what he seas fit for the Co. We have got some 50 or 60$ worth of stuf on the road for our men. We ar looking for it evry day from Nashville. The boys ar all well and a cicking. Is thare any land thare now that is not taken up? If thare should be any let me know for thare is one of the boys in my co. that would like to get a peace thare somewhere. I dont think of anything more at present so I will close with lots of love to all. I will write again some time again in

59. Earlier in the war General Oliver Otis Howard, from Maine, had fought in many of the major eastern battles. He was criticized for being surprised by General "Stonewall" Jackson at Chancellorsville and for activities during the first day at Gettysburg. He was then shifted to the west and fought around Chattanooga during this period of time. He later commanded a corps in march to Atlanta, and, in July of 1864, became commander of the Army of the Tennessee.

60. General Joseph Hooker likewise was censured for unsuccessful efforts in the East against Lee's forces. He badly bungled the battle of Chancellorsville and shortly thereafter was replaced by General George G. Meade and "exiled" to the western theater. Taking two corps with him he fought magnificently at the battle of Chattanooga and later around Atlanta.

the first of the weak. I will send in this the photograph of my bead
fellow, C. L. Dunham.

To Mrs. Jane Dunham

Lookout Station, Tennessee, March 22, 1864

I take this present opportunity to drop you a few lines to let
you know that I am yet among the liveing and well and harty. I
received yours & Hercys letter several days ago and have not had
time to answer it untill now. I was glad to heare from you and to
heare from you in person and to heare that your health was good.
We had rather a hard trip comeing down heare, it was so wet and
mudy. We arrived heare in the woods on the 10th of this monthe.
We have got comfortable houses fixt up again foure in a house, but
I dont know how long we will stay heare. We have a fire place in
our cabin, but it smokes so that we can hardly stand it some times.
That is about like soldering all through. For my part I have got
enough of soldering to do me if the war should come to a close
right away, but I dont see mutch prospect of it closeing very sone.
I wish I could get a furlow but that is out of the question. Thare
was an order isued to give them and I put in fur one but the order
was countermanded before they had hardly chance to make one
out. I dont mutch expect to get one while I am in the service unless
a reb hapens to give me one. It has ben very cold heare for several
days. It snowed all last night and all day today and the snow is now
all of a foot deap. I have hurd people talk about the suny South but
for my part I have seen enough of it to satisfy my appetite. We are
campt right at the foot of Lookout Mountain whare Gen. Hookers
forces went up when they took it. It is about one mile and a half to
the top. I have ben to the top. It is a grand sight a person can see as
far as thare eye can reach. You said in your letter that thare was
four or five of the boys of the 39th got married. I am a thinking if
thare is many more vetran Regt comes back thare, thair wont be
know sight for ous poor fellows when we get back. I dont think of

anything more to write so I will close with lots of love. Give my best respects to all of your folks, C. L. Dunham.

To Mrs. Simeon H. Dunham

Lookout Station, Tennessee, March 27 and 28, 1864

I received yours and Hercys letter this morning and though it came yesterday but I did not get it untill this morning for I was out on picket yesterday. We was out so far the boys did not fetch the letters and I was out some five miles. I said I was on picket—I was not on picket, I was patroal guard on the railroad. Your letter found me harty as ever. I tell you what it does me lots of good to heare that you was all well. It seemd to me all day that thare was a letter waiting for me in camp. It is most splendid wether heare today but we have had awful wether for the last weak. Back last Wednesday the snow was a foot dan a half deap. That is in the suny South, but when they talk about the suny South *I cant see it.* But we had got our houses fixt up comfortable so that we did not mind it mutch. But if it had come a little sooner when we was on the march it would have give ous fitz. I tell you what we have got just as good a thing as we want heare. We wont go on duty only about twice in a month but we have six ours drill evry day except saturday and Sunday, but that wont hurt ous I guess. I tell you what we ar liveing high now days on stors that the captain bought with Co. funds. I will just name over the things; Potatoes, that is irish potatoes, too lbs. of crout [sauerkraut] satch as the dutch like, and I tell you what I have got to be a pretty good dutchman, a lot of onions, one barrel of pickels, a lot of dried appels, and one barrel of green appels. So we ar just liveing in the hight of our glory now but I tell you what we neaded some sutch stuff when we got down heare for we was rather gaunt. We was a good deal like grayhounds. I got a letter from Chester a day or too ago. He is well and harty. I will stop wrighting for now and finish in the morning for it wont go out untill tomorrow anyhow.

[March 28] Monday morning all alive and a cicking. It looks

as iff we was a going to have sum more rain. We had dress parade last eavening and the order was red that we ar to have five hours drill evry day excepting Sundays and they would drill ous then iff they dard to. A curced nigger is thought more of than a soldier in this war. I tell you what is the fact. I have seen a black devil a rideing in an ambulance that could walk just as well as not and a poor soldier come along that could hardly drag one foot after the other and wanta ride but know you cant ride you ar just glaging off.[61] I have seen that with my one eys. I would like to see Hiram. I could tell him a little how the thing went heare and I would bet he would not care about enlisting. I will close for this time as I have fild the sheat and breakfast is about ready. So I will close with lots of love to all and a right smart for yourself. . . . You can send a few stamps once in a while iff you ar a mind to for they ar hard to get down heare. The socks that you said you was a going to send will come tip top, C. L. Dunham.

To Mrs. Simeon H. Dunham

Lookout Station, Tennessee, April 3, 1864

I just received your letter of the 26th. Words cant tell how glad I am to heare that you ar all well. I am well and harty excepting the tooth ache. I have had it for two or three days. My face is swolen prety bad. I have not mutch time to write for the mail goes out at 11 o clock ane it is after tenn now and I just got your letter. Today is a splendid day but it has ben very bad wether heare for some time, cold and weet. The 23 of last month the snow heare all of one foot an a half deap. The rebs say that we brought the cold wether down with ous. We have got a splendid camp fixt up warm and nice. Hoskins got heare Monday. I got the stockings that you sent and the candy. You could not have sent any thing that I kneed as mutch as I did the socks. I have not seen Hoskins to talk with him yet since he got back, for I was on duty when he

61. This was Laforest's expression for "goofing off" or trying to receive a special privilege by faking injury.

came. He brought the socks to my tent. The boys ar all well that you ar acquainted with. I am sory to heare that Jane is sick again. Thare is preaching in camp now. We have preaching now evry sabath when the wether will admit. You see our church is a large one all out dores. Capt Perry is going to be major. I gues Major Flinn [62] is in Cropseys place as Leiutenant Colonel. I have got some appels over a stewing. I tell you what we ar a liveing high about these times. We draw soft bread part of the time now. I will have to come to a close or I will be to late to get it in the office so as to have it go this morning. You must not wory about me for I am doing well, have a plenty to eat and a plenty to ware. I will close with these few lines with lots of love to all and a good big lot for yourself, C. L. Dunham.

To Mrs. Simeon H. Dunham and Hercey

Lookout Station, Tennessee, April 8 and 10, 1864

I received your letter this morning of the first and am glad to heare that you ar all well and to heare that Jane is getting better. I am harty as ever and able to eat my rations evry time. We ar haveing very bad wether heare cold and weet. Today it is cold and windy. Ma I received a letter from you last Sunday and sat right down and answered it. I guess you will think it is a great letter but I tell you what I did not feal mutch like writeing for I had had the tooth ache or face ache for three or four days. In the first place I had the tooth ache and then it went into my jaw and my face sweld up all most as big agin as it ought too be and it paind me so that I could not sleap nights or set still day times, but it brouk inside yesterday so I am all OK now. You better believe that I put in a nights sleap last night that counted. The Doctor said it was caused by a cold. I have not hurd from Chester for some time but I think I will get a letter from him in a day or too. The report is that they

62. Major Thomas H. Flynn, from Winchester, Illinois, enlisted on February 27, 1864—the day that Lt. Colonel Cropsey resigned. Major Flynn remained with the 129th until he was mustered out on June 8, 1865.

are agoing too consolidate the 11th & 12th corps so iff they do we will bothe be in the same corps. Thare is talk bout our a going to Ritchmond and I would not wonder if we did before long, but thare is know knowing whare we will go when we leave heare. David Harbeson is the name of the person that that photograph was taken from. You said you thought you had seen him. You might have seen him thare in camp at Pontiac. He is the one that I traided coats with. I gues you remember about it. You said in one of your letters that Hiram said that he wished he was down heare martching with me. He might as well wish himself most anywhare else. Iff he wants to know how soldering goes let him take about 80 Pounds on his back and march threw the mud all day and then lay all night on the weet ground, then he can tell what soldering is like. For my part I dont want any more of my Brothers in this show. Thare was too of ous came out in this war and that is enough. Iff it is as our Colonel reckons it, we have only a year more to stay in the service. The way he reckons it if sutch a part of the Regt. have not got a furlow then we will be allowed our furlow time and thare has not any whare near half got them yet. I dont think of any thing more to write so I will close with lots of love to all. Sunday morning the 10th. I wrote this letter day before yesterday and calculated to put it in the office yesterday but I forgot it. I am well and have just got done my breakfast so that I am OK. Good by for this time with lots of love, C. L. Dunham.

To Miss Hercey Dunham

Lookout Station, Tennessee, April 17, 1864

As I have got through the usual Sunday morning inspection I take my seat on my bunk to drop you a few lines to let you know that I am yet alive and a gruntting. I received your & Mas letters of the 10th this morning. I tell you what I am glad to heare that you ar all well. We have had splendid wether heare for several days. It is most a splendid morning this morning. It makes me wan to be at home Sundays. Seme the most like Sundays heare of any place we

have ben since we have ben in the service, but after all it dont seme
like home. Thare is preaching in camp now, but I thought I must
answer your letter right away. We had grand review last Thursday
by General Tommas [*sic*] [Thomas], Hooker and Butterfield.[63]
Thare was something like eight thousand Soldiers present. General
Thommas is a going to visit our camp tomorrow. I tell you what
we have to put on the stile heare.[64] Have to have our boots blacked
when we go on guard or inspection, if we dont we catch fits. I tell
you I have not had a letter from Chester for some time but am
looking for one evry day. The boys ar all well hear that live in
them digings when they ar at home. Would that I could be in old
Ill. guiding a plow about these times but that cant be. I think thare
will be a forward movement pretty soon iff the wether holds good
for a weak longer. I am ready for my part for iff they ar ever a
going to thrash out the rebs I wan to get doen with it and then go
home, iff I live through it. Captain Perry is not a going to get the
Majorship and the hole co. is glad of it. Capt. Hoskins will be our
Major. Perry would get it iff it went by vote. I will have to come
to a close for I declare I cant think of anything more to write. I
would fill the sheat ful of trash but then what would it amount to.
It would not interest you at all, so I will close with lots of love to
all. Your loveing Brother Laforest, The Soldier Boy.

To Mr. Simeon H. Dunham

Lookout Station, Tennessee, April 26, 1864

I have a few lesure moments so I will improve it in writeing to
you to let you know that I am alive and a cicking. I received your,
Mas and Her. letter last Saturday and I intended to answer it
Sunday, but Sunday I was detaled to go on picket and did not get
in untill yesterday noon and I was so sleepy that I put it off untill
now. We ar haveing splendid wether heare now all though it is

---

63. Brigadier General Daniel Butterfield of the U.S. Volunteers.

64. Laforest is referring to the fact that more than any time since his 1862
enlistment the soldiers are required to be in proper uniform all the time.

rather hot. I have not mutch time to write for the drums ar beating for guard mounting now and it will soon be time for company drill. I expect we will get paid off the first of next monthe and iff we do I will send you 60$ by express. D. Robinson [and I] is a going to send together.[65] I got a letter from Eugene a day or too ago. He was well when he wrote. We have three drills a day company, Batalion, Briggade and once a weak Division drill. That dont give ous mutch time for play. I tell you I have not herd from Chester for some time. I gues he did not get my last letter. I sent you a paper last weak, the Nashville *Times*. I presume you have got it before this time. I dont think we will stay heare but a little longer but for my part I dont care what I am the rest of my time. The boys ar all well. I dont think of anything more to write and it will be time for drill by the time I get it in the office so I will close with lots of love to all. We ar now the 1st Brigade, B Division, 20th Corps, C. L. Dunham.

To Dear Ones at Home

Lookout Station, Tennessee, May 1, 1864

  I have not mutch news to write only to say that I am well as usual. I received your letters of Apr 22 yesterday. I am glad to heare that you ar all well but sory to heare that you have so mutch bad wether. We ar haveing splendid wether heare. The treas ar all leaved out and I tell you what it makes me feal as iff I ought to be at home to work. We ar haveing quite a revival in our Regt. We went to work and put up a church—it is about the size of our house. I attended meating this morning and a prar meating [*sic*] [prayer meeting] last eavening. Thare was to be preaching at three o clock this afternoon but we have got marching orders. We ar to leave heare tomorrow sometime in the morning I expect, whare too I know not (as usual). We expected to get paid off this weak but it is not likely we will now. I was in hopes we would for we have a

---

65. Laforest and Delos Robinson plan to send their money together in one sum.

good chance to expres it heare. You spak about my reenlisting. I think when I surve my three years out I have don my share. I think the Regt will reenlist within three or four months but they may all go in to a man but myself and I know I shant.[66] Thare is a large army heare now. You must not wory about me, it wont make it a bit better. I will take the best care of myself I can, and I think I am prety good at it. I will stop writeing for a little while till we have dress parade and maybe we will find out some thing what is to be don or whare we are a going.

I will comense again. We have had Dress parade. As we was draw up in line we had a prare by our Chapplain. We ar to leave heare in the morning at six o clock. You nede not think strange iff you dont heare from me in some time but it may be so that the mail will go through. The boys ar all well and harty. I dont think of anything more so I will close with lots of love and good wishes. Your loveing Son & Brother Laforest. Heare is a pease of laurel root that I got off of Lookout mountain and I whiteld it out as it is now. I thought I would send it for a curiosity. I would say a few words more but it useless for me to express my fealings.

66. Laforest will make many references to the fact that when his enlistment is up he is going home whether any one else does or not. He is not being disloyal to the cause or expressing disappointment with the generals or administration; rather he is exercising the privilege of every soldier to complain whenever he wants to.

LAFOREST'S JOURNEY THROUGH GEORGIA

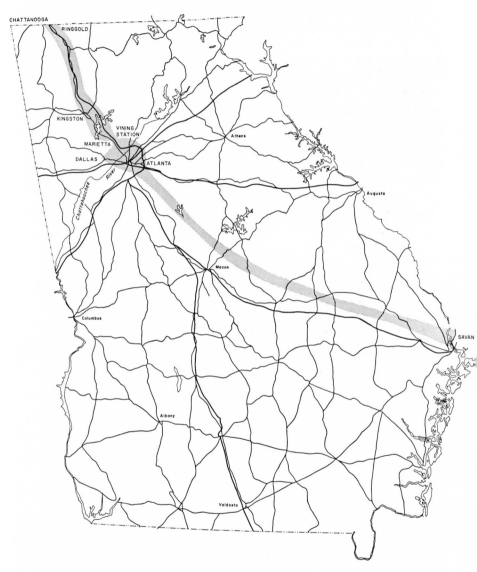

The Georgia Letters
May 4, 1864–November 11, 1864

To Mr. Simeon H. Dunham

Camp near Ringgold, Georgia, May 4, 1864

As we have campt for the night I take my pen in hand to drop you a few lines to let you know that I am well and harty. We have marched too days and laid over one. We are prety close to the rebs. We ar with in eleven or twelve miles of the rebs main force. We will have a fight soon may be tomorrow and maybe not so soon, bout dont give yourselves any uneasyness about me. It may be my lot to fall but it wont be any worse than a good many others. Delos Robinson is leaning aginst a tree and writeing to his father. We ar haveing splendid wether for marching. The boys ar all cherefull and redy to give the rebs the best we have got—that is of blue pills. I dont think of any more to write so I will close with lots of love, your loveing son, Laforest.

To Mrs. Simeon H. Dunham

Camp in the Woods, Georgia, May 9, 1864

I take the present opportunity to drop you a few lines to let you know that I am well as usual and I hope thes few lines will find you all well. I have not mutch news to write but a few lines may be better than non. We came heare whare we ar campt now day before yesterday. It is a very nice place for a camp. It is so shady. I wrote to pa the other day and I said in the letter that we expected to have a fight the next day but we did not have it and I dont know when we will have one. For my part I dont think the rebs will make mutch of a stand. We have an awful[1] army heare. The Second Division of the Corps had a bit of a fight with them [rebels] yesterday nite but a little wase from heare.[2] We could

1. By the word "awful" Laforest means large, tough, and superior to the army of the enemy. In this context awful is used to indicate what his army could do to the rebels.

2. From May 8 to 14 the Illinois 129th fought many minor engagements with the Confederate forces. The battle was joined in earnest on May 14 and lasted through the next day before victory was secured.

heare the musketry plain. The day we came heare we drove the rebs pickets in. Thare was only too shots exchanged. Our Regt was in the advance. It is my opinion that the war will close within six months. I think the fighting will be done in four months. Chester is about a mile from heare. He is in the first Division. It is very warm and dry down heare but thare is plenty of good water. I got J.[oseph] Wilsons letter day before yesterday. James Hayes is bak at Ringole at the hospital. He was sent back for he give out on the march. Soldering is know place for him. One thing he has not got grit enough—he gives up to quick. You must not wory about me, I have a plenty to eat and a plenty to ware. I will answer Josephs leter as soon as I get a chance. The boys are all cheareful as usual. I dont think of anything more to write so I will come to a close with lots of love to all and a good big lot for your selfe, your loveing son Laforest. I dont know whether this will go or not but I thought I would write.

To the Dear Ones at Home

Camp in the Field, Georgia, May 20, 1864

I take this present oportunity to drop you a few lines to let you know that I am a live and well all though we have had rather a hard time but I stood it very well. We had a fight last sabath. We went in the fight a bout one o clock and it lasted till long in the eavening. Our Briggade charged on a fort and we took it too. Thare was four pieces of cannon in it and the rebs used them on ous prety well. I *tell you* we was under fire four days but we clerd the rebs out prety well. Corporel Howard was kild. You knew him I gues. He was home on a furlow last summer. Frank Barr had too fingers shot off of his right hand. Thare was one kild and eight wonded in our company. Delos Robinson and Roo . . .[3] came out all right. For my part I dont care about getting in to annother one but I thought shure we would have annother pull at it again yesterday. We was scaremushing [*sic*] [skirmishing] all day yester-

3. It is impossible to read this word. I suspect Laforest is referring to Aaron Ross.

day. We have ben driveing them right before ous ever since last Sunday. Lieutenant Smith of Co. A was wonded, I dont know how bad. Martin Deloune [4] was wounded. One bullet came close enough to me to cut my coat on the joint of my left sholder and one went through my hare. My hat fell off and as I grabd it one took me through the hare and top of my head. Thare was forty seven kild and wonded in the Regt. I have thought of it a good many times since however a man escaped for the rebs was so well fortified.[5] The same place had ben charged on five times before by our troops and they could not take it, but we took it the first charge but it was a horible sight. I wont wright any more about it for you will see it in the papers, so I will come to a close. I dont know whether it will go or not. We got the news heare that thare would not any letters go for thirty days, but the post master said we might right some and maybe they would go through. I suppose it will go as far as Nashville anyhow. So I will come to a close with lots of love to all, Your loveing Son & Brother Laforest. I have not had a letter from any of you for some time. The reason is the mail wont come to ous.

To Mrs. Simeon H. Dunham

Camp near Kingston, Georgia, May 22, 1864

I have not mutch news to write but thought I would drop you a few lines to let you know that I am well and harty. Peter Shafer is

4. Martin DeLong was a fellow soldier from Esmen Township. He enlisted on August 2, 1862, was wounded during the conflict, and was mustered out on June 8, 1865.

5. This is an impossible sentence and there is no way to improve it by simply inserting punctuation marks. However, it is an appropriate sentence for this letter. This was the first real taste of battle, blood, and bullets that Laforest has had since enlisting in September of 1862. He had always arrived on the scene a few days after the action took place, or left shortly before it started. Now he was in the thick of it all and it excited him beyond anything before in his life. He jumped all over the place in this letter; scribbled short choppy sentences; and, at times, made little sense. An incredible thing has happened to Laforest: he has met the enemy on the battlefield, flirted with death, and emerged not only victorious but alive. I think he always anticipated immediate death in his first real encounter with the enemy; such was not the case and he was both relieved and excited.

discharged and he is a going to start for home tomorrow. He belonged to my company. We have ben campt heare three days. I wrote you a few days ago bout our fight but I dont know whether the mail goes through or not. The boys in our part of Ill. came out right side up with care. If reports ar trew I think the war will soon close. The report is heare that Grant has given the rebs a good thrashing and I know we have heare. We have just drove them before ous. We expect to take up the line of march tomorrow for whare I know not. Delos Robinson wrote to his father a day or too ago but he dont know whether the letter will go through or not. So if Pa seas him he [Delos] would like for him to tell him that Delos is well and harty. We ar haveing splendid wether heare even though it is very hot in the middle of the day. I have not got a letter from any of you for some time. I got one from Eugene a day or too ago. He was well when he wrot. Chester is well! He was in the fight last Sunday the same time I was. We went in to the fight about one o clock and it lasted untill dark. I dont think of any thing more a present so I will close with lots of love to all and a big lot for yourself. Your Loveing Son, LaForest. Peter Shafer is a going to take this through. He lives acrost the river somewhere.

Just received your letter of the 10th glad to heare that you ar all well. I would like some mush iff you can send it just as well as not. I tell you what a person has to look out for himself or he will get so lonely that he wont know himself. It is now about too o clock and I tell you what it is prety hot. Know more at present so good by.

TO MRS. SIMEON H. DUNHAM

Camp near Dallas, Georgia, May 30, 1864

As I have a few leasure moments I will improv it in droping you a few words to let you know that I am well, that is tolerable. I have ben under the wether for a while so that I was back at the hospital but I came to the Regt last eavening. The boys have had rather a hard time while I was back, some fighting to do and building brestworks.[6] Peter Lawler was kild on the 27th. He was shot right through by a sharp shooter. Good had his right hand shot off by a shell. Once in a while thare is a ball comes over whare we are but the boys have got so that they dont care mutch about them. We are now back in the third line of battle. I think we will play the rebs out in a few days, but they have got a strong hold. Dont wory about me it wont make it a bit better. I thing the war will close this summer iff Grant is successful on at Ritchmond. We have taken a great many prisinors and they all say that iff we play them out heare they mite as well give up. We took one prisoner yesterday and he said thare officers said we was getting short of men but he said he could se it in a diff rent light now. He said he should think when General Sherman got to the head of the army heare that his command would create attention and make the kingdom right whole [7] (prety good for the rebs). Delos Robinson, A. Ross, and the rest of the boys that you ar acquainted with ar all right. I will close with these few lines for we dont know what minute we will have to fall in, so I will come to a close with lots of love to all and a big lot for yourself. Your Loveing Son Laforest.

To Mr. Simeon H. Dunham

Camp in the Field, Georgia, June 7, 1864

I just received yours, Mas & Hurceys letter. Words cant begin to express how glad I am to heare from those that I love dearly and to heare that you ar all well. Your letter found me well and as harty as a buck. We have had very bad wether for some time. It is just commenceing again to rain. We came heare whare we ar now last eavening and I tell you what we work like good fellows to a makeing breastworks. We expected the rebs would pitch on to ous

6. In late May the 129th was busy in many engagements. The men had operated on the line at Pumpkin Vine Creek, and participated in the battles of Dallas, New Hope Church, and Allatoona Hills from May 26 to June 5.

7. When Sherman takes over complete command of the army in northern Georgia, they will take Atlanta. This act should end the war and lead to an immediate reuniting of the Union.

last nite but it seames that they thought is would not pay. We have not had any fighting to do only scourmishing since the 15 of last month but we have ben under fire most of the time. We ar now within about 25 miles of Atlanta but thare will be some hard fighting before we can get thare. Evry thing seams to be very quiet heare now. It has been over three weaks that we have ben under the roare of the cannon and musketry but now we cant heare eather only once in a while, but we would not have to go far to set up a roaring. I have not even ben scrached yet. You must not believe evry report you heare. If I get wounded I will write wright off or have some one else to do it for me. The boys that you ar acquainted with ar all well. I have not scene D. Finley for a day or to, but the last time I saw him he was up and a comeing. I have not sen Chester since the last fight so that I dont know whether he came out all right or not. I got a letter from Eugene some time ago but I have not had time to answer it. We never know heare when the mail is a going out untill a few minutes before it startes—would that the war was brought to a close. For my part I dont care about going in to annother one but iff they call uppon ous I am ready to do my share. I dont think of anything more to write for news is scarce down heare so I will come to a close with lots of love to all. Your Afft. son, Laforest.

TO MRS. SIMEON H. DUNHAM

Camp in the Woods, Georgia, June 12, 1864

The word just came that the mail would go out at six o clock so I thought I would drop you a few lines to let you know that I am yet alive and well. We ar campt now whare we was when I wrote last—have ben heare a weak tomorrow eavening. We ar haveing awful wet wether. It raining most of the time. I received yours, Pas & Her. letter of June 1 a day or too ago. I am glad to heare that you ar all well. Thare is three or four Dunhams in the Regt. Thare is not mutch fighting going on, none only scourmishing and cannadeing. I am sory to heare that Jane is so poorly. I should have written to her again but to tell the truth I dont feal like writeing when I have a chance. Would that this war would come to an end. Never did I know what it was to be away from home untill I came into the armey. Oh, I hope Eugene or Hiram wont come in to the army. Thare was too of ous came and that is enough out of one family. Dear mother you said you would be so happy to heare that I was one of the ones that was converted in our Regt. Ma I feal as iff God was on my side. It useless for me to try to express my fealeings. I have resolved to be a christon the rest of my life. Doo pray for me. I know you do Pa & Hercey too. I must. . . .[8]

To Mr. Simeon H. Dunham

Field near Marietta, Georgia, June 23, 1864

I have not mutch time to write for the mail is a going to go out in a few minutes but I thought a few words would be better than none. I am well and harty. We had a bit of pull at the rebs yesterday but as good luck would have it we only got one wonded in our company.[9] The rebs charged on our left and I tell you it was a splendid sight. The rebs came up three lines deap but they went back quicker than they came. I tell you what thare was a pile of them slaughtered, they went in all directions but after all it is awful. Lieutenant Edgington got a letter today and it stated that Jane was dead. I hope it is not so but I feare it is, but if it is so I trust that she is better off than in this world of trouble. I got a package from Ma & H. a few days ago with some mush in it. I am glad to heare that you ar all well. I have not hurd from Eugene for some time but I suppose it was my falt for I did not answer his last letter for some time after I received it. You must not think streange becose I dont write any more for I have not got but a half sheat more of paper, so I will draw to a close with lots of love to all. Your Afft. Son Laforest.

8. The last sheet of this letter is lost.

9. The battle mentioned here is the small engagement at Kolb's Farm on June 22.

To Mrs. Simeon H. Dunham

In Field South of Marietta, Georgia, June 29, 1864

I received your and Pas letter of the 17th. I am glad to heare that you ar all well. Your letter found me well as usual but I was sory to heare the sad news of Janes death, but I trust that she is better off than in this world of trouble. We have had very warm wether heare for the past weak. It looks as if we was a going to have some rain. We have ben heare whare we ar now about a weak. We have got strong entrenchments maid, or brestworks rather. As neare as I can find out we have got the rebs in a pen so that they have got to fight and in our own works. We ar looking for an attack evry minute but iff they do try it thare will be more dead rebs than ever was hurd of. Chester and myself have ben together most of the time for the last three or four days. He is well and harty. I wish we was both in the same Regt. You cant immagin how mutch good it does me to get with him. Somehow it seams as iff I was clost to home. If I ever get out of this show a live and well, I never will get so far from home but what I can heare the first rattle for dinner. I think I will know what home is when I get back. All of the boys that you ar acquainted with ar all well and harty. We ar between the rebs and Atlanta. I will have to come to a close for this is all of the paper I have got and dont know when I can get any more so that when you. . . .[10]

To Miss Hercey Dunham

From a Camp 3½ Miles South of Marietta, Georgia, July 2, 1864

I have not mutch to write but I will do the best I can. I am well as usual. It is now about six o clock in the eavening. Looks as iff we was a going to have a wet night. I just received your & Mas letter of the 24th. I tell you what thare was a roaring heare this morning.

---

10. The rest of this letter is lost but, seemingly, unimportant as he was bringing it to a close.

Our cannon opend on the rebs this morning a long the hole line. As far as we could heare thare is heavy scourmishing most of the time, but it dont amount to mutch. Thare is lots of rebs comeing in and giveing them selves up all the time; that is in the night they come out on the scourmish line and whistle and our boys answer them and then in they come. This I know myself! Thare was too hundred and fifty came in all in one squad day before yesterday just before daylight. Chester is all right. Have you got a letter from him lately? He said he had written but had not got an answer yet. He did not know but what you did not like his letter very well for he said he joked you some in it, but I told him he ned not think any sutch thing. You wanted to know whether I got any letters from any of the G.[urnsey's] or not. Sertunly. I will tell you I got a letter from Katie a day or too ago. I get one from her about once a month but I dont get any from Joan. Katie said that she had been wanting to come down to our house but thare folks wer so buisy with thare horses that she could not get ane to go any whare with. I hope you all will have a good time the fourth. You must have a good time iff thare is any sutch thing in the book. You mgt. [*sic*] [might] so as to have some to spare me. I expect High [11] will be sky larking around with some of the wegen gals. I expect High thinks that I dont do right in not writing to him any more than I do, but when I write to one it is for all so he must not feal bad about it. I dont think of any more so I will come to a close with lots of love to all, your loveing Brother, Leaforest. A word to Hiram. Dear Brother, I feale as if I ought to say a word or so to you. Hiram we may not live to meat in this world again but I hope we will meat in a better one. I mean to say a word or to and you must not feal hard of it—that is to be a good boy and do all you can for Pa & Ma in thare old age and I will asshure you that you will never be sory for it. Just take my advice. Some times I get so uneasy when I heare about boys enlisting for feare that you will, but do stay at home. If you knew how the word home sounded to me you would know something about it. High write me a good long letter. I will close

11. High is the family nickname for brother Hiram.

for this time. I will write you a good long letter before long when I get time.

To Mrs. Simeon H. Dunham

Camp in Woods near Marietta, Georgia, July 9, 1864

I have a few leasure moments to spare so I thought I could not improve it better than to drop you a few lines to let you know how I am getting along. I am well and harty as ever. I am writing under a tree. It is awful hot heare now. We ar with in tenn miles of Atlanta. We can see it from heare. Did you have a good time the fourth? I will tell you what kind of a time I had. I will commence at the morning of the third. Our forces out flanked the rebs so that they had to leave thare position, so we advanced the morning of the third. We had advanced about two miles and we run on to the re-treating column of the rebs. We wer on a hill and so were the rebs and our forces ran up to pieces of cannon and opend on the rebs. But it was not long before the rebs sent over the shell a whorling. You had better believe we hugd the ground about that time, but as good luck would have it they did not do mutch hurt. Kild one in the Co. and wonded a number in our briggade but the rebs thought it would not pay to stay thare long so they put on the double quick. So we went about five miles and went in to camp, the rebs right in our front in breastworks. So the morning of the fourth both sides opend with cannon and I tell you what thare was a roaring that beats any fourth that I ever saw or hurd of before. But long in the afternoon the rebs put out again and so we followed, stopt tramping once in a while and gave them a few shells and musketry. We expected too have rather warm times before night but we did not. We went in to camp about sun down and then we drawed three days rations and I tell you what they give ous big ones to. The boys were grumbeling the next day about thare load —this makes three days we have ben heare at this place. Chester is all right. We ar with one another most of the time. His Regt. is only about a half of a mile from heare. When we came heare we had orders to fix up our camp so we have got it fixt quite comfortable but I dont know how long we will stay heare. H. wanted to know how long I was at the hospital in her last letter. I was thare about a weak, I had the army quick step. I suppose you know what that is.[12] I dont think of anything more to write so I will close hopeing these few lines will find you all well. So I come to a close with lots of love to all. Your loveing son Laforest. Chester received his letter. I have not got the paper that you sent yet.

To Mr. Simeon H. Dunham

Camp in the Woods north of Atlanta, Georgia, July 16, 1864

I have not mutch news to write but maybe a few words will be better than non. I am well and harty as ever. I have not got a letter from any of you since the second of this month. It was dated the 24th of last month. I got a leter from Eugene day before yesterday. He was well when he wrote. It is very hot down heare in the wilderness through the day, but rather cool nights. We have ben heare tenn days on this ground but the flanks ar buisy a moveing in. We have to out flank the rebs out of thare works. It would be an awful thing to try to carry thare works by storm. In fact it cant be don they could kill all that was a mind to try it. We tried one charge and that is enough to satisfy me all though we carried our point. I think iff Grant is successful thare at Ritchmond the show will wind up this winter, but iff he is not three more years wont any more than see the end of itt. But iff ole Abe [President Abraham Lincoln] is [re] electted I think it will help it along considerable. I tell you what kind of a man [13] [he is]; he spoke a number of times in Nashville last winter. He is death on rebs. Chester is all right. I have not seen him today but he was well yesterday. I gues I will go and see him this afternoon. The boys ar

12. Diarrhea.
13. Without warning, or a transitional phrase, Laforest has left Lincoln and is back on Grant again.

MOVEMENT AROUND ATLANTA

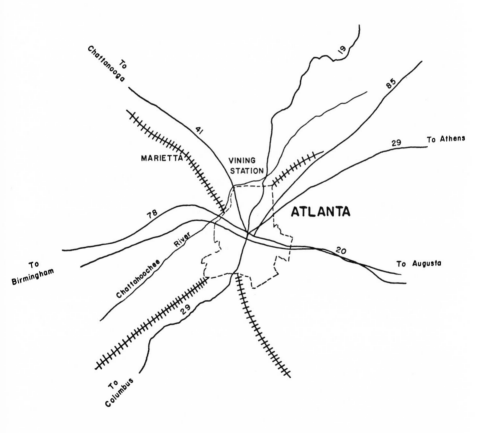

all well that you ar acquainted with. Thare is talk that they ar a going to let all enlist again that came out when we did so as to be at home at the time of the Presidential Election so as to vote, but I gues it is more talk than sider. But for my part three years is long as I wan to surve at once. Any how I dont think of anything more to write that amounts to anything so I will come to a close with lots of love to all and I hope these few lines will find you all well. I remain your afft. son Laforest. I presume I will get a letter from some of you this eavening. Thare is considerable talk about our corps a going to Richmond. Some of the officers think that we will within too weaks and if we do and go by the way of Louisville, I am a comeing home if thare is any such thing but I dont mutch think that we will go thare but we cant tell one day from annother whare we will be the next. We have prair meating evry eavening now while we ar in camp and it is a dooing a great deal of good.

To Mrs. Simeon H. Dunham

Camp in Field within two miles of Atlanta, Georgia, July 23 and
24, 1864

I take the present oportunity to drop you a few lines to let you know that I am still alive but I am some what under the weather. Wednesday we had an awful fight about too miles from heare [in] whitch our Regt. took an active part,[14] but we came out victorious after three ours hard fighting. Thare was three of our corps in the fight—the 4, 14, and 20 corps. Our company got cut up prety bad but not as bad as I was afraid it would be. Our briggade was right in an open field. We wanted to gain a hill so as to fortify and the rebs thought they would not let ous but they had to come to it. The field was literaly covered with dead and

14. By July, 1864 Atlanta was completely ringed on the east and north by Union forces. On July 22 the famous Battle of Atlanta began as General John Hood unsuccessfully attacked the forces of the Army of Tennessee under General James McPherson.

wounded rebs. Our Briggade got around so as to have a cross fire on them it was a hand to hand fight. The rebs had three lines of battel and we had only one for all of our forces had not got a crost the river. I thought for a while our boys would have to give back but know they went in for all that was out and hurld the rebs back with a rush. The rebs attacked our skirmish line about an hour ago and drove them in a ways. I thought shure they was a going to try ous annother pull, but they did not come. The scourmishers have-ing it right and left with our Second Brig. Now the shels ar bursting over our heads all the time. Iff you can read this you will do well for I cant help starting once in a while when a shell bursts so clost and loud. Thare is a continual roar all of the time but we have got good breastworks so that they cant do ous any harm. Thare was two kild and nine wonded in our company. Lige Sclosher is one of the wounded and the doctor thinks it is doubtful whether he gets well. He was shot in the head. He is the only one that you know that was hurt. I was not in the fighting myself for I was sick but I stood back on a high hill so that I could see it all. I have had a high fever all day today so that I dont feale mutch like writeing, but I thought I must drop you a few lines to let you know how I was getting along.

July 24th. I had to stop writing yesterday afternoon for the rebs keept attacking our scourmishers an we thought they was a going to attack ous. Had our guns in hand but they did not come, so I will finish this morning. I feale some better this morning. Thare one of them consing shells just bursted right over our heads, but they cant do ous any harm. Our batterries can through shells into Atlanta from heare iff they ar a mind to. We ar only too miles from the city. As soon as our forces get around on thare flank they will have to get out in a hurry. That is the only way that we can get them out of those works. They ar awful strong. I have not hurd from Chester since the fight so I dont know whether he is all right or not. I got yours & H's letter of the 9th several days ago. I have not got the paper that you sent yet. I dont think of anything more this time so I will come to a close with lots of love to all and big lot for yourself, Your afft son, Laforest.

To Miss Hercey Dunham

Camp within two miles of Atlanta, Georgia, July 28, 1864

I received your letter of the 16th too or three days ago and I got one of yours that was written July second the same day. Thare was a long time thare that I did not heare from any of you and it seamed like a long time. I tell you the rebs ar prety quiet this morning. They ar shelling ous pretty mutch all of the time but I gues they ar takeing a rest this morning, but thare shelling dont amount to anything. Our Brigade is now in the reserve but I supose we will go on the front line in a day or so. For my part I would just as soon be on the front line as to be in the rear. It is a most splendid morning this morning. We had a nice shower last eavening so it is quite cool now. Would that I could have ben at home with Eugene. Oh, wouldent I enjoy myself! I dont believe thare could be a happier beaing than me if I was at home now, and know what I do. But what is the use of thinking of any sutch thing when we know it is out of the question, but still it would come up in a persons mind now. Three months we have ben whare the roar of cannon and musketry is kept up all of the time, night and day. I tell you what I am tierd of it. Hurcey, would that I could express my fealings as I would like to. Iff thare is any place that a person ought to lade a criston [*sic*] [lead a Christian] life heare is the place, for a person dont know what time he will be cald up for to leave this world of trouble. Iff it should be my lot to fall, I hope and trust that we will all meat in a better world whare wore and troubles are know more. The boys ar all well that you are acquainted with. I have not seen Chester since the fight so I dont know whether he is all right or not. I dont think of anything more this time so I will come to a close with lots of love to all, Your Loveing Brother Laforest.

To Mr. and Mrs. Simeon H. Dunham

Camped on field two miles southwest of Atlanta, Georgia, August 2, 1864

I dont know whether I will have time to finish this or not before we get orders to moove but I thought as I had nothing to do I had better drop you a few lines, if I did not write mutch. I am as harty as ever again. We ar now on the extreme right of the army so that we ar able to moove at any moment. It is the quietest heare of any place we have ben for the last three months, some scourmishing but not to amount to mutch. We expected an attack last eavening but the Joneis,[15] as we call them, did not come. If they do come they will go back prety well scattered I will bet, for we have got strong works and plenty of big guns. The 16 & 15 corps had a hard fight prety mutch on the same ground that we now ocupie. The rebs charged our boys five times but evry time they went back quicker than they came. The rebs loss was estimated at 9 thousand. Our boys had know breastworks at all nor the rebs, just took the woods for it. The old 20th Ill. is prety mutch used up. The rebs got all around them so that they took prety mutch all of them prisinors what they did not kill. Some twenty escaped; I believe I saw one of the boys yesterday. I have not seen Chester since the fight of the 20th, so I dont know whether he is all right or not. The rest of our corps is a round in the senter yet. Thare is only our Division around heare. We have lost old Gen. Hooker— [16] he left for some reson I dont know what. I tell you what we hate it but we cant help it. Some think that we will leave heare before long. They think that Gen [Hooker] has gon to see about takeing ous away for he said that our corps would not go in to Atlanta. I

15. The Yanks referred to the Rebs as "Johnnys" and that is the word intended in this sentence.

16. At the Battle of Atlanta General James McPherson was killed and replaced by General O. O. Howard. This appointment was taken as an insult by Hooker, who had commanded and fought brilliantly in Tennessee and Georgia since his fiasco at Chancellorsville. Because he was overlooked in favor of Howard, he asked to be retired.

will have to come to a close for the mail goes out at eight o clock and it is about that time now. I have never got that paper that you sent. I maid out to get a quarters worth yesterday. I will find you all well with lots of love to all. I will close for this time hopeing that I will heare from you tonight when the mail comes in, Your Afft. Son Laforest.

MR. HIRAM DUNHAM

Camp near Atlanta, Georgia, August 6, 1864

I have just eat my breakfast and it is pretty cool and I had nothing to do so I thought I would drop you a few lines. As you know that I am a live and a cicking, I am as harty as ever again. We have got around to our old place again in the senter of the army. It is pretty quiet this morning but if you was heare you would not think it quiet that is iff you had just got heare, but it seams still to ous for we have hurd so mutch of a roaring for the past three months. Thare is three rebel forts right in our front heare. We have got very strong breastworks and so have the rebs. Our works and tharn ar about one hundred rods apart. Thare flags ar floating on thare works and so ar ours on ours. We had to stick pretty clost to our works yesterday for the shells wer flying pretty thick both ways. Our scourmishers are out about fifty yards from our works. Thare is a good many balls come a whisling over our works but they dont amount to mutch. We have got so use to them that we dont pay mutch attention to them. Our [railroad] cars run right up to our works yesterday and hooted thare for a half of an hour just to tanalize the rebs. I looked for the rebs to open on them with thare cannon but they did not. Chester is all right. His Regiment was not in the fight on the 20th. I gues I will go over and see him as soon as I get this letter written. Hiram, how does the reaper run this season? I tell you what I wish I could be thare to help you along with your work, but what is the use of my wishing when I kno it is imposible. How does the horses look? How many hogs have you got? Have you got the same dog that you had when I left? I want you to write me a good long letter and let me know how things look in general, write anything and evry thing. Camp is in a compleat roar. You will wonder what for I gues. Wal I will tell you. We ar a going to draw one days rations of soft bread. We have only twenty men for duty in our company now. I tell you what it dont take up the round that it did when we left Pontiac. The boys ar all well that you are acquainted with, excepting Lige Sclosher. He is back wonded. Lige's father was heare to see ous the other day. He looks about the same as ever. I have not got a letter from home since the one that was written the 16th. The mail did not come yesterday but it will be in before this goes out. I dont think of anything more to write this time so I will close with lots of love to all. Your loveing Brother Laforest. The mail has come in but know letters for poor me. I have not got the paper yet that our folks sent and I never will I gues. I maid out to get twenty five sents worth the other day.

To Mrs. Simeon H. Dunham

From Camp near Atlanta, Georgia, August 10, 1864

I have a litle lesure time. I will improve it in writeing you a few lines to let you know that I am well and harty as ever. I received your and H's letters of July 23 and 30th both together a day or two ago, so you can see how the letters come. A. Ross got a letter yesterday from home and they said that they had seen some of you and that you wer all well. I tell you what I am glad to heare that. It is very hot heare but we ar haveing a shower most evry day now, see that it makes it beter on the wonded. We have to keep prety clost to our works for the bullets come over prety thick some of the time, but we have got so ust to them that we dont mind them mutch. Thare was prety hard shelling heare yesterday but the most of it was on our sid. The rebs did not fire but a few shots. Our forces wer shelling Atlanta. The rebs have got a strong hold heare but we will rout them out before long, iff we have to dig them out and blow them up. Chester is well. He was over to see me yesterday and I was over to see him the day before. The boys ar all well that you ar acquainted with. I thought John G[uernsey] was a regular coperhead. I hope they will get to drafting thare and bring some of them down heare and see how they like it. Ile bet they would sing a different song in a little while. Thare is considerable talk of the Ill., Ind., & N.Y. troops a going home to vote this fall but I cant hardly see it myself, but I hope it is so but that would be too good a thing for a soldier. Dear ma you must not wory so about me for it wont make it a bit better. I know it is hard but iff it should be my lot to never get home, I hope we will all meat in a better world whare wars and parting ar know more. I wrote Hiram a letter three or four days ago. I have not got the paper that you sent yet and it ant likely that it will get through. Iff you send any more dont fasten the ends up, and put on it soldiers paper and it wont cost so much, but I gues you had not better send any more. Just send a sheat in your letters when you write. You mite send a bunch of envelope, for them we cant get. I dont think of anything more so I will close with lots of love to all. Your loveing Son Laforest. Tell Hiram they cant draft him and he must stay at home and be a good boy.

To Mr. and Mrs. Simeon H. Dunham

Near Atlanta, Georgia, August 14, 1864

I received your letter of the 6th last eavening when I come off of the scourmish line. I tell you what I am glad to heare that you ar well. Your letter found me well and harty. I was on the scourmish line night before last and yesterday was relieved. Last eavening the rebs thought they would rush on ous but we soon gave them all they wanted. I tell you what the bullets flew prety thick for awhile but none of our boys got hurt for we stuck clost to our pits. Thare was one in Co. E kild heare in camp. The boys in camp thought shure the rebs was a going to charge our works but they did not get that far, iff they intended to. Thare is not mutch cannonadeing going on today. The rebs ar doing all that is don.

The scourmishers ar keepeing up quite a lively fire but that dont amount to mutch. Thare was six reb dissenters came into our Regt. last night. I am glad that Eugene is comeing home. I wrote him a letter a day or too [ago], taint likely he will get it iff he comes home. I was over to see Chester this morning. He is well and harty. We ar haveing very hot wether hearn now but have a shower most evry day. Delos Robinson will be on the scourmish line tonight. He is well and so ar the rest of the boys that you ar acquainted with. The rebs seme to be bound to stick to this place if we captur them. I hope they will hold heare for a while longer. I think if they do thare wont many of them get away. We ar building a fort a little to the left of our Regt. I gues we will get it don tonight. They ar a going to put som larg guns in it. I dont think of anything more to write. What I have written dont amount to mutch but may be it will be better than non. Hopeing these few lines will find you all well, I come to close with lots of love to all. Your loveing son, Laforest. We have a plenty to eat such as it is. Hard tack, beaf and pork. We dont get any vegitables at tall.

To Miss Hercey Dunham

Near Atlanta, Georgia, August 21, 1864

I have not mutch news to write but I thought I would drop you a few lines to let you know that I am yet alive and well. I have just eat my breakfast and am now writeing on my table. I presume you would like to know what kind of a table I have got, wal I will tell you. It is a hard tack box and my seat is the ground. We had quite a rain last night so that it is quite cool this morning. It is very still this morning to what it is as a general thing. We maind a bargin with the rebs to not shoot at one another on the scourmish line so that thare is not mutch musketry, but our Atlanta express, as we cal it, is a going this morning. I will tell you what our Atlanta express is. It is a large cannon that throes a 32 pound shell into Atlanta every 10 minutes. We have got the rebs last railroad cut off that runs into Atlanta. So they will have to get up and dust prety soon or be captured. Oh, if we can just captur this army heare the war would soon come to an end. The rebs got around to our rear and cut our cracker line so that the mail did not come for four days, but it is all right now the mail came in yesterday. I thought shure I would get a letter but it was not my luck to get one, but I am in hopes I will get one from you today. It was two years yesterday that I enlisted. Have you seen anything in the papers that all of the troops that came out in that call that I cam in ar to be discharged next June? That is the news heare. I hope it is so. I long to see you dear ones at home again. Dear sister, it has ben a trying time for me since I left home. It is uncommon to see a soldier cry but the tears will come when I look back to what is past and gone. Dear Sister, I dont know how I will every pay you for your kindness in writeing to me, but iff I ever get back you will neve want for a kind and loveing brother. Iff I do say it I dont see as soldering has maid me a bit hard harted and I have often thought I was prety tender harted. I tel you what, I know what home is now. Thare never was a boy had a better home than ous boys. I have often thought about when I use to do rong and Pa or Ma would talk to me and tell me I would be sory for it some day, but I could not see it then or pretended so but I can see it now. Oh, I hope Hiram will be a good boy and stay at home and help Pa & Ma all he can. I will have to come to a close for the want of rom. Chester is wel, he was heare yesterday. I wont mail this until the mail comes in.

[on a separate short page] It is now half past 2 and the mail has not come in so I will have to mail this for the mail goes out at three o clock. Something tells me that when it does come in I am a going to get a letter from some of you. It has ben raining most all day. I went to meating this morning at 10 o clock. Capt. Culver preached; our chapplain has got his discharge since meatting. I have ben reading me bible most of the time. I tell you what it is a great deal of comfort to me. I was looking over some of my old letters the other day and in one of them you wanted to know what kind of a fellow Goud was. If you wan to know write me in your next and I will tell you. Love to all and a good lot of it to. Your loveing Brother Laforest.

TO MR. AND MRS. SIMEON H. DUNHAM

Near Atlanta, Georgia, August 25, 1864

I have not mutch to write but will drop you a few lines to let you know that I am well. I received your letter of the 15th day before yesterday. I should have answered it yesterday but I was on picket, came off last eavening. I have just eaten my breakfast. Maybe you would like to know what I had for breakfast, wal I will tell you. Nothing very enticing but we dont grumbel as long as we get a plenty. Sutch as it is hard tack, beaf, and coffee, plenty of sugar. We will have beans for dinner. We ar haveing very hot weather now but cool nights. It is very quiet this morning know cannonadeing going on in heareing. We maid a bargain with the rebs not to shoot at one annother heare on the scourmish line unless one side or the other went to advance, so it makes it mutch plesanter. We will stand and look at one annother not more than 25 rods apart, look at one another like some wild beasts. The report is that our corps is a going to be put on the railroad to guard from Chattanooga to Atlanta, for the one hundred days mens time is about out.[17] I tell you what I hope it is so I aint the only one that hopes so ether. We have seen all the fighting that we care about, but if we ar cald uppon or if it is our lot we ar ready to give the rebs the best we have got in the shop. James Hayes came up to the Regt. yesterday. He has ben back at Chattanooga at the hospital. He has not ben in a fight yet. He sais that Eliza Sclosher is getting along first trate. I wrote H. a letter three or four days ago. When you writ again if you ar a mind to you may send me a little black thread. You can put it in with a letter. We cant get any sutch thing heare at all for love nor money for our Sutlers are not allowd to come up. You nede not be afraid of my enlisting again for I shant. If I get through my three years all right, I think I can be contented at home. I dont think of any thing more to write so I will come to a

17. A reference to the Union soldiers who would be discharged within one hundred days. It would be senseless to send them forward when, supposedly, they would be leaving the armed forces shortly.

close hopeing these few lines will find you all well. With lots of love to all I close for this time, Your loveing son Laforest. Heare is a secesh bill it may be kind of a curiosity if you have never seen any.

To Miss Hercey Dunham

North of Chattahoochee River, Georgia, August 29, 1864

I received your letter of the 20th last eavening. I am glad to heare that you ar all well. I am well and harty as ever. You will se by the heading of this that we have got on the north side of the River again. We ar at our old traid again not exactly guarding the railroad but guarding the railroad and the base of supplies. Thare is only one Briggade on this side of the river. The rest of the corps is just on the other side well fortified. Our *Brig.* is strung out just a company in a place, and that ant all. We ar occupying the rebels works. We evacuated our works before Atlanta the night of the 25th. The rebs followed us sloly but did not dare to rush on to ous for feare that we was trying to get them into some trap. I supose as neare as I can learn the main army is a going around in the rear of Atlanta on strike for Macon. General Slocum [18] is in command of our corps and is in command of the railroad, so I think we will stay on the railroad this winter. We have got first trate summer quarters fixt so that we are just at home again. You wanted to know if I knew if my birthday had past. I was so buisy heare or something else that I was thinking it was on the 26th of this month, but I know now when it was. It has ben over four months since I have had my clothes off to go to bead and the bigest part of the time had to keep our shoes on. We ar haveing splendid wether but rather warm all though we have plenty of shade. We ar right in the heavy timber. In fact Ga. is all woods and hils. You said calico was 50 cts a yard. Ant I glad I havent got a woman. I wish you had some of the coffee thare that we waist. Our Company wast enough evry

18. Brigadier General Henry W. Slocum.

day for a half dozen families. I have not seen Chester for several days. He is about three miles from heare. I don't think of anything more to write so I will come to a close with lots of love to all. Your loving Brother Laforest. Tell Hiram I want him to send me a chew of Prarie gum. He can put it in a letter.

TO MR. EUGENE H. DUNHAM

Two miles north of Chattahoochee River, Georgia, August 31, 1864

I received your most welcome letter day before yesterday. It found me all O.K. I hardly know what to write for news has plaid out but I will do the best I can. I was on picket yesterday, was relieved last eavening. I tell you what it seams like old times to be orn picket whare we have not got to be a looking out for a bullet evry second. We have got tip top summer quarters fixt up once again. I have got a table to write on. Maybe you would like to know what it is maid of. Wal it is maid of crates and my chare is my bunk so you see that I am right in town (all but what lacks of it.) We muster today for eight months pay, but I dont know when we will get paid off. Thare is a rumer that we will get it pretty soon, but thare is so many grapevine reports (as we call them) that a person cant believe anything that he hears. I wrote to Hercy three or four days ago and stated in the leter that we had fell back from our works before Atlanta fell back to the river. The 1st & 2d and part of our Division is on the South side of the river well fortified. This is a going to be the base of supplies heare. Our Briggade is strung out a Co. in a place. I think our corps will be strung out on the railroad this winter for thare has got to be a very heavy guard for the rebs ar doing the best they can to cut off our cracker line. They seme to think that is thare only salvation, but I dont think they can come it. Some of the boys ar shouting for all that is out thare ar pitching horse shoes and one side scunked the other so they wer haveing quite a time over it. Our Briggade band is a playing and it sounds very nice. Sems a good deal like America once again.

You said you wished that I could be at home next summer (dont I though) and I think I will be. I think the war will be closed one way or the other this winter, but I dont pretend to be any proffit but that is what I think of it. I wish they would let our Regt. come home to the election. I would bet that some of the copperheads would get what they would not like. I believe I could level my gun on one of them helish traitors. I must say beter than to level it on a reb down heare. I dont think of any thing more to write so I will have to come to a close. Delos sais he cant think of anything to write this time but sends his best respects to you and the rest. I will write to Hiram in a few days and maybe I can think of something to write by that time. When I get a thinking of home (and that is very often) it is all I can do to sit still long enough to write one letter. I close hopeing to heare from you soon again, love to all, Your Afft. Brother Laforest. John Carol,[19] I gues you knew him, he was our fifer. He went in a swiming two or three days ago in the river and took the cramp or some thing else and drowned. He undertook to swim a crost. We have only 28 men for duty in our company now. When we left Wahatchie we had something like 70 men, so you can see what we have ben through.

To Mr. Hiram Dunham

Two miles north of Chattahoochie River, Georgia, September 3,
1864

It is a raining its best licks and I have got to go on picket tonight but then I gues I can stand it. When some of you write again send me some postage stamps. It takes the last one I have got to send this. I have received the envelops too or three days ago. I dont know how far this letter will go for old Wheler [20] has cut the

19. John H. Carroll entered the service as a recruit from Rook's Creek Township on August 14, 1862. He was promoted to Fife Major before he met his untimely death swimming.

20. Confederate General Joseph Wheeler who conducted numerous raids near Atlanta and opposed Sherman's march to the sea. The twenty-eight year old general earned the nickname of "Fighting Joe"; he was considered by many to be one of the greatest of all Southern cavalry leaders.

railroad at Cowen [*sic*] [Cowan] Station, Tenn. So we dont get any mail today. They want the bloody 129 up thare to tend to thare caces. In the fight of the 20th one of the staff officers told Colonel Case that he stood right by the General and they thought the rebs would drive our Regt. for the rebs came up with three lines of battle and wer pitching in to our Regt. harder than any other part of the line and the General stood watching and he sais thale hold them, thale hold them, thale hold them! That 129 is true as steal. I must brag a litle on the Regt. Know mor at present, Laforest.

To Mr. Hiram Dunham

Camp near Vining Station, Georgia, September 9, 1864

I will try and answer your letter this morning all though I have not mutch news to write. I am well as usual. It is very warm and sultry this morning, raind all night. I have got some good news to tell you, Atlanta is ourn took it yesterday with nine hundred prisinors. I was at the generale headquarters when the dispatch came that it was taken. I myself and five others was detald to go down the river about four miles and the General was writeing out the pass for ous to get through the picket line when the dispatch came to him and he told ous what the dispatch was and said that we nede not go for Atlanta was ourn. So it saved ous from a rough old trip. I gues the 2nd & 3d Briggades of our Division wer the first in to Atlanta. Thare has ben annother hard fight south of Atlanta and the rebs got an awful thrashing. Sherman cut the reb army right in too so that he drove them in all directions. I think if Grant gets Ritchmond now the fighting will be prety mutch over, but I am afraid that it will be a good while before he gets it. I think our Briggade will ether go into Atlanta or go back further on the railroad. The report is that thare has got to some troops from heare go back betwene Bridgeport & Chattanooga. I hope that our Brig. will go. Our quartermaster went into Atlanta yesterday and staid all night and has just got back. He sais that our corp is all in thare but one Briggade. So I think we will stay heare at the river. It is a

first trate place heare so I would just as soon stay right heare for
one year as anywhare if we have got to stay in the service. I will be
on picket tonight but I dont mind picketing heare. You said that
John Guernsey was a regular copperhead and carried a revolver.
He dont amount to mutch any how. A barking dog wont bight
very often. I dont think I wrote to him last some six months ago
and he has never answered it and I dont care whether he ever does
or not. I know that he got the letter. I hope I can be at home next
summer to help you farm. I tell you what wouldent you and me
make the fir fly. You said you raked off of the reper this summer.
You must be a good deal stronger than I am now. I am getting a
little fraid that you will win that bet off of me but you must give
me a year to gane my strength when I get home. I dont believe that
I can lift more than half that I could before I left home. You see
our work is different heare to what it is thare. It is hard on the eys
as well as on the body heare. Some time I will tell you of one hard
time that we had. We was three days without anything to eat only
a little beaf and that they had to lean agunst tufens to knock it
down. We use to stell corn from the officers horses but that was
not mutch, for the horses did not get mutch but then that dont
amount to mutch. It is all past and you dont mind what I have ben
through. It is what is to come but then I gues I can wether it
through if some reb dont pick me move. I have not seen Chester for
some time. I went over crost the river day before yester to see him
but his Regiment had gon out on a scout so I did not see him. That
photograph that he sent H. dont look mutch like him or at least I
dont think it does. I will have to come to a close on the account of
room.

Hi. Do you go to see that gal? Lets see what is her name? Wal I
gues I have forgotten. You must take good care of yourself and
write me an other good long letter. You cant thing how mutch
good that letter does me. One thing I came near forgetting to tell
you, we drew one days rations of light bread last eavening, lots of
love to all Laforest.

To Mr. and Mrs. Simeon H. Dunham

Camp near Vining Station, Georgia, September 9, 1864

I have not mutch of any news to write but a few words may be better than non. I am well as usual. We ar still at the same place that we have ben for the past two or three weaks, but expect to moove to Atlanta evry day. It is now about eight o clock in the eavening but I go on camp guard at tenn o clock, and as Leiutenant Edgington our first Leiut. is a going to start for Nashville tomorrow in a leafe of absente, I thought I would send a letter by him to mail thare for I dont think our mail that we write heare goes further than Chattanooga for Old Wheler is on the railroad somewhare. We have not had any mail for two weaks. I tell you what we ar looking anxiously evry day for it. Time pases off so slow again when we dont get our mail regularly. I tell you what. The rebs got annother good thrashing down heare if reports ar true and I think they ar. I dont think the reb army will amount to mutch heare any more. We captured lots of big guns in Atlanta but the most of them wer spiked but one thing about it they wont get to use them on ous any more. I tell you what we ar all anxious to heare how the draft is comeing of. When we get five hundred thousand more troops out the rebs wont be know whare. We ar haveing splendid wether heare all though rather hot in the middle of the day but very cool nights. I think the nights ar cooler heare as a general thing than they ar in Ill. The boys ar all well that you ar acquainted with, I believe. I have not seen Chester for some time. I supose he is in Atlanta though. It was too years ago yesterday that we was mustrd into the United States service as a Regiment. We can count months instead of years now any how, but I dont think the war will last that long. I think it will end this winter sometime. Any how it is out of the question for the rebs to stand it annother summer. We havent had any news heare for sometime. We ar all anxious to heare how they ar getting along at Ritchmond. I dont think of anything more to write this time but I will write in two or three days again and sooner iff I get a letter from any of you. So I will close hopeing these few lines will find you all well and lots of love to all. I remain Your loveing Son Laforest.

To Miss Hercey Dunham

Camp near Vining Station, Georgia, September 13, 1864

I have not mutch to write but I will do the best I can. I received yours and Mas letter of the 27th of last month yesterday. We have not had any mail untill yesterday for about two weaks. I tell you what time pases off slow when we dont get our mail regular. It is a splendid morning this morning. We ar haveing prety cool nights heare now. We ar still at the same place that we have been ever since we came this side of the river. We have got a tip top camping ground but we expect to moove back to the river or to Atlanta evry day. I under stand that our corps is assignd to guard the railroad. I hope it is so. We ar all anxious to heare how the draft is getting along. The report is heare that thare is to be 25 out of Esmen but I cant see it. I would like to have the privilege to draft a few thare. Ile bet I would cleane out a few of them copper heads. I dont think they would be copperheads long after they got heare. I wish they had drafted from the start and not of let a man enlisted and then thare would not have ben so many trators in the north now. You said you had maid Guss's wife a visit. How do you like her? How does Guss and his Father get along this summer? I think John had better go and enlist in the rebel army, he thinks so mutch of old Jeff. Any one that talks as he does is nothing but a right down coward. Iff he was going into a fight when the guns began to crack he would run like a deer. When a fight comences the sound of the guns sound like poping corn but when you get parly in to it you would not know that thare was a gun fierd for it is one continual roar. I have not seen Chester for some time. I sen that photograph before he sent it to you, but I dont think it looks much like he does now for he has got whiskers on his face now, that makes considerable difference. I will have to put soldiers letter on this for I am out of stamps. I got the tobaco that Pa sent yesterday.

Was ent you somewhat surprised when you found out that I used it? I have used it for a year or about that. The way I comensed useing it, I use to get so lonesom that I did not know what to do with myself. I took up chewing. I get so lonesome now some times that I hardly know what to do with myself but I can stand it a good deal better now than I could when we first came out, but I gues I can stand it for not quite a year more. I dont think of anything more to write so I will come to a close with lots of love to all, Your loveing Brother Laforest.

To Mr. and Mrs. Simeon H. Dunham

Atlanta, Georgia, September 17, 1864

I take my position on the ground this morning to write you a few lines to let you know that I am still alive and well and that we have arived at the great city that thare has ben so mutch talk about. We broke up camp yesterday morning at four o clock and got heare at Atlanta about noon. It is not as nice a city as I expected to find it. Our shells have riddled it considerable, but after all it never was a nice place. It has ben a great manufacturing place for the rebs. I just came down a few minutes ago from a reb fort. I tell you what they had to heare some big guns. I expect the rebs thought we never could get them out. They had awful strong works. It would have ben imposible to have charged them and taken them. Even if we had taken them we could not have held them for they ar in such shape that they would have had cross fire on ous from all directions. I received your letter of the 7th day before yesterday with thread in it. I am glad to heare that you are all well. We had a pretty hard march comeing heare yesterday for it was so hot and dusty. Thare was a good many give out but I maid out to wigle through. Some of the boys a cleaning off the ground for our camping ground. I am writeing this in a hury for I expect the Regt. will move pretty soon on to the ground. Then we will have to go to work at our tents. The boys ar all well I believe. I have not seen Chester for some time but I gues I will see him before many days for they ar campt (that is his Division) on the north side of town and we ar on the south side of the great city. I dont think of anything more to write now. I did not expect to rite mutch when I comenced but I thought I had better write a little for maybe that I would not get a chance in to or three days again, so I will close with lots of love to all, Your loveing son, Laforest.

To Mr. and Mrs. Simeon H. Dunham

Atlanta, Georgia, September 22 and 23, 1864

I hardly know how to comence a letter for I have know news to write but I will do the best I can. I am well as usual. We have got first trate quarters fixt up again so you see that wear right at home and board at the same place. I was around through the city the other day. It is not mutch of a city all though it covers over a good deal of ground. The houses ar very scattering but it has ben a great manufactoring place for the Rebs. When they left heare they distroid an awful sight of propity. They had any amount of guns and ammunition of all kinds that they could not get away so they burnt it up. They had lots of plateing for gun boats that they could not get off. To make our shanties we tore down houses some nice ones to. That is the way the army does. Sherman's shipping most all of the women and children through into the reb lines. Thare is any amount of them that dont wan to go but Sherman dont propose to fead them. He oferd old Hood [21] to keep them heare if he would keep the road from being tore up, but Hood would not do that. Then Sherman said that he would not fead them. He would ship them through the lines and let them fead them selves. I saw Chester day before yesterday. He is well, but blind after the sun goes down. Thare is a good many that way. Thare is four or five in our Regt. the same way. I dont know what is the cause of it unless it is caused by over exertion. You nede not send any more paper or envalops for I have got plenty of both. Lieutenant Edgington

21. General John Bell Hood replaced General Joseph E. Johnston as commander of the Confederate Army of Tennessee defending Atlanta in July, 1864.

weent to Nashville and he brought up a lot for the company. Thare was an order isued to give furlows and we drew cuts in our company to see hoo should go and I drew a ticket that said furlow so I had one maid out and the Colonel signed it and the rest that had put in and sent them to the Briggade commander and he would not sign them. I would like to know what they wan to isue such orders if they dont intend to give them. I know one thing if I live to see my time out they can go on with thare rat kiling but they cant get me in to it, know way they can fix it. I dont think of anything more to write so I will come to a close with lots of love to all. Your loveing Son Laforest. I have just ben out of the tent to get a cigar. Major Hoskins is treating the Regt. to the cigars. I tell you what I am puting on the stile with a cigar in my mouth.

Sept. 23d. I was to late to get this in to the office yesterday. I am all right and a kicking this morning. I have not got a letter from any of you since we came heare; we came heare on the 16th. I am in hopes I will get one today, by for this time, Laforest.

TO MISS HERCEY DUNHAM

Atlanta, Georgia, September 27, 1864

I received your letter of the 17th yesterday. I tell you what I was glad to heare that you wer all well. We came heare the 16th of this month and I had not got a letter from any of you untill yesterday, that is since we came heare. I am well and harty as usual. We had two inspections Sunday and had grand review yesterday by Gen. Slocum (our corps commander). I wish you could see how we have got our shanties fixt up. Thare is four in a shantie. The eaves ar about four feat high and our roof is our purp tents. We carried the boards about a mile—tore down houses to get them. We have two bunks in one end one above the other and we made a table out of ruff board and each one made a stool and we have places (or hooks rather) to hang our guns up and other things fixt according. So you see that we ar right at home and board at the same place. We ar haveing very cool nights heare now. I expect

you have had a frost thare before now, but I am glad to heare that
the corn is out of the way. If it would that I could be thare to help
husk it, but I supose that is imposible. I had to stop writeing to eat
my dinner. Delos and Aaron Ross got dinner ready so I stopt
writeing and eat my dinner and now I will tell you what we had
for dinner. First place I will tell you that we had light bread, next
pork (was not fresh though by a good wase), and beans, and plenty
of suger & coffee, that we allways have a plenty of. I went over
to Milers Battery, the Battery that Joseph Barr and Bill Brown
belong to. I was glad to heare that Frank got home again. Frank
was a good soldier. I miss him very mutch he would do most anything for me. If he comes to our house again tell him to write to
me. I got one letter from him when he was on the campain, but I
had not time to answer it right away and when I did get time I
thought it would not be likely that he was at the same place when
he wrote, so I did not write to him. I will tell you the names of the
boys that ar in my tent. First Delos, he is my bead fellow, A. Ross,
and Henry Hallam—he lives when at home over thare by Mr.
Nighs. Thare is some talk of a fall campaign this fall but the most
of the officers think that thare wont be any but if thare is one they
think our corps will stay heare. I hope so at any rate. Thare is a
pretty good sign that our Division will stay heare for they ar
takeing all of our best mules out of our teams and turning them
over to other corps. For my part I dont think the war will last
longer than spring at the furthurest. I think all the rebs ar holding
off for to see how the Presidential election is a going. I hope old
Abe will be elected. I know he would if they would give the
soldiers a vote. The war would have ben ended before now if
them cowardly whelps at the north had of kept thare mouths shut
and not have doen anything else. Ile bet that they will get paid
back in thare one coin when the soldiers get back to America again.
Chester was over to se me last Sunday. He was well and harty. He
has ben at night so that he could not see at all after sundown but he
has got over it now; it was caused by over exertion. I suppose that is
what he thinks was the cause of it. I did intend to fill this sheat full
but I wont have time to before the mail goes out. Now about what
I wrote you about. He [Frank] was allways first trate to me and in

fact to the hole company. The boys have wished him back any amount of times for they dont like the orderly that we have got now. But he [Frank] is one of these kind that is noted for these houses of ill fame and has a dissease that he never will get over by so doing. But as a man other ways he is a first trate fellow. I think that is enough so that you will know what kind of a fellow he is. I have not got any more time to write in order to get this to the office so that it will go this afternoon. So I come to a close with lots of love to all, your loveing Brother Laforest the sugar boy.

To Mr. and Mrs. Simeon H. Dunham

Atlanta, Georgia, October 1, 1864

Once again I take the opportunity to drop you a few lines to let you know that I am well. I have not mutch news to write but a few words may be better than non. We are not a going to have any drill today for it is Saturday. We have three drills a day other days through the weak. I expect they will drill ous till the day our time is out, when we ar in camp this way. I dont know whether this will go right through or not for the report is that the railroad is tore up and I gues it is so, for we have not had any mail for three or four days. I hope we will get it today. Time pases off slow when we dont get our mail. We had a heavy rain last night but it is a splendid morning this morning. We ar a going to have an election in our Regiment today just to see how the Regiment would go if we was whare we could vote. I know if I was whare I could vote I would give old Abe a lift. I would just as soon vote for Jeff Davis at once as to vote for McClen [22] runing on the platform that he is, but I think thare is know doubt but what old Abe will get elected. I know he would if the soldiers all had a chance to vote. I dont think thare will be any general move heare this fall, but thare is a going

22. General George Brinton McClellan was the Democratic Party candidate for the presidency of the United States in 1864. The Democrats were willing to negotiate peace with the South and were not demanding a return to the Union as a condition of peace; the soldiers—and many others—abhorred this show of moderation.

to be heavy raiding don on both sides. We have the report heare that old Wheler is captured and a good share of his forces. I hope it is so. I tell you what the rebs ar on thare last legs. Thare is know doubt about that. I hope it will close this winter if not before so that I can be at home next summer. I believe that I could go at farming now with good pluck if I only had the chance, but that litle word if is in the way. We ar a going to have grand review of the hole corps some time next weak by General Tommas. I tell you what it will be a grand sight for a person to stand and look on, but I dont care mutch about it. For my part thare is little to mutch marching about it, and you know that I am one of these kind that dont like to work very hard but thare is one thing surtain that I ant a going to hurt myself while I am in this show if I can help myself. We have preaching in camp now most evry eavening. We have not ben paid off yet but ar expecting to be most evry day, and if we ar paid of I wont draw but a little of the money heare. The pay master sent some allotment rols to the regiment and we can sign any amount of our pay that is comeing to ous and hoo we wanted to send it to and they will send the money from Springfield right to the one that we want it to go to. I think it will be safe that way. Whenever we do get paid off I will write you right off and let you know the amount that I send. I will send some thing like 128 dollars. I dont wan to keep but a little with me for it is not very safe. We drew some sanitory [23] the other day. We drew some craut [24] and onions. I tell you what it was tip top. I dont think of anything more to write this time so I will come to a close with lots of love to all. Your loveing Son, Laforest.

To Mr. and Mrs. Simeon H. Dunham

Camp on Chattahoochie River, Georgia, October 9, 1864

　　I have not hurd from any of you for a long time and I presume you have not from me. We have not had any mail to amount to

23. The correct word is stationary.
24. Kraut or sauerkraut.

anything for three or four weaks and I tell you what I am a getting uneasy, but then I have to put up with it. Major Hoskins is a going to start home in the morning on a leaf of absence and he said that he would take all of the letters that we was a mind to wright. I presume you have hurd all about the moove ments of the army before this. Our corps is at Atlanta that is the most of it. Our Briggade wheare a guarding the railroad bridg. We came from Atlanta to heare a weak ago yesterday and I tell you what we came on the double quick for they expected an attack thare at the bridg and thare was only one Regiment heare then. We have got prety well fortified heare now so that I think it will take a prety large forse to get ous out of our works. We have got tip top shanties fixt up again and I tell you that we nead them to for it has ben cold enough the two last nights past to sit by a good fire and the wind has blown yesterday and today like it dose thare some times. I would think shure that we was in Ill. if I could look off and see nice level ground, but it is just the other way heare. All that a person can see heare is mountains and they ar all coverd with heavy timber. We have not ben paid off yet and I dont think we will be for some time. For my part I dont care whether we get paid off this winter or not. If a person had all the money that he could cary heare he could not by anything. I tell you what this country is prety well cleand out. It is a compleat wilderness. How is the draft a getting along or ant they drafting in the North? We have not had any news down heare for a month or more. We are all anxious to heare how Grant is a getting along. I think the reb army heare is on its last legs. I hope it is at any rate. I have not seen Chester for some time but the last time I saw him he was well and harty. We have had weet cold wether heare for some time. It raised the river so that it washed the railroad bridg out, but they have got it about fixt again. I guess the cars will run over it tomorrow. I have run ashore for some time to write. I cant think of anything to write that will interrest you any at all. If you ar a mind to you may send me a pare of gloves by Hoskins if he will bring them. I think he will. I would like to have a pare of boots but they would be too mutch trouble for him to carrie them I expect, so you need not

bother about them. It would not be safe to send them through by
express. Thare is one thing that I came neare forgetting to tell you.
Henry Courtice [25] sent me some tobacco, maid me a present of it;
sent it through by one of the boys that belongs to Co. G. that was
at home wonded. I dont think of anything more to write this time
for the fact is I dont feale like writeing today. I am in hope that we
will get some mail fore long but it looks rather skaley. I dont mutch
think that Hoskins can get through. Know more at present, hopeing these few lines will find you all well. I will close with lots of
love to all, Your loveing Son, Laforest.

To Mr. and Mrs. Simeon H. Dunham

Camp on Chattahoochie River, Georgia, October 18 and 23,
1864

I comence this leter not knowing when it will go, but I
thought I would write and have it ready when the mail got to
runing again. I received to letters from you, Hercy & Hiram a day
or too ago. I tell you what it does me lots of good all though they
were a good while a comeing through, but I am glad to heare that
you wer all well when you wrote. I am well as usual, can just make
the hard tack git. We ar haveing splendid wether heare just cool
enough to be plesant. We have got a fire place in our shantie so you
see that we ar right in town. One of the letters had the gum in. I
tell you what it tasted like old times. I hope I will be thare next
year by this time or before. I think the war will wind up this
winter. The rebs ar know doubt on thare last legs but then it may
last a year yet. But if it should wind up this winter I dont think we
will get home mutch before our time is out for they will keep a
large army in the field till the thing is all settled up. The 79th Ohio
(a Regiment in our Briggade) held an election the other day and
thare was only five votes cast for McClen and the rest for old Abe,
and it is a large Regiment to. I tell you what it does me to heare

25. The only thing about this gentleman that I was able to uncover was the
correct spelling of his name—Henry Curtis.

that some of them copperheads wer drafted. I think it will learn some of them a lesson. If it hadent ben for them the war would have ben ended now. I hope J. Wilson can com heare. I would like to see him first trate but I don't think they will give them thare choice, but they may. Hercy said in her letter E. & H. said if they could get 2000$ that they would go as a substitute. If I was thare they could not pille up mony enough in a weak to get me to go for one of the cowardly whelps. What is money any how to the pleasure of home. Hiram dont know what home is yet and I dont think thare is many that does that has not ben tried in some place like this. For my part I do not know how the word home sounded untill I came into the army, but to heare the word spoken or think of it strikes a tender spot. I tell you would that I could see Hiram and have a talk withe him. It dont seme to me that he can be so cruel to leave home and leave Pa with out any help at all. He promised me when I left that he would stay and do the best he could. I should be in misery the rest of my time out if he should leave but it dont seme posible that he can be so cruel. I will have to stop writing now for I am detald for fatigue duty on loading cars or something of the kind.

Oct. 23. I will comence again this morning for the mail is a going out today. I received a letter from Ma & Hercy last eavening. It was maild the 10th. It was not dated in the in sid. We had a big scout last weak. We was gon three days. We had a tip top time. I tell you what we made the chickins, sheap, and hogs git. I got a cantean full of molases. It goes off first trate on hard tack and then we take hard tack and pound them up fine and mix them up with water and bake it and it goes first trate with a little molases on it. It is most a splendid morning this morning. Our Briggade band is a playing and it sounds tip top. Henry Streter [26] is a going to start home on a furlow to morrow if nothing happens. I may send this by him. We have not got our pay yet but I think we will get it this

26. I found no record of a Henry Streter in Company C or any company in the 129th. There is, however, a number of persons named Streator around the Livingston County area: I would suggest that the correct spelling of the name is Streator and not Streter.

weak some time for part of our Briggade is ben paid off. The way that they are paying the troops they give them a check for the money. I dont know exactly how they do mark it, but it is done so that thare is know danger of looseing it. I presume you have seen Major Hoskins before this time. I wish that Wilson could come to our company. I tell you what it would do me good to see him, but I am afraid they wont give them thare choice. What was done with that forty that A. laid his county order out on? [27] If I ever get back I mean to get that 80. I tell you what if I ever get back I calculate to go to farming and stay thare. I have got enough of romeing this kind any how. The boys ar all well that you ar acquainted with, I believe. It is some time since I have seen Chester so I dont know how he is getting along. The bughl has just blowed for company inspection so I will have to stop writeing for now.

We have got through inspection. It did not take ous but a few minute. I don't think of anything more to write this time so I will have to close. It is rather doubtful whether this gets through for the rebs ar tareing up the road most evry day. Know more at present so good by this time with lots of love to all, Your loveing Son, Laforest.

To Miss Hercey Dunham

Camp on Chattahoochie River, Georgia, October 28 and 29, 1864

Once again I take my pen in hand to drop you a few lines to let you know that I am still alive and well and can eat hard tack as well as ever. I received your and Mas letter of the 15th last eavening. I tell you what it done me lote of good to heare that you wer all well and getting along all right. I had just got in off of a foraging expedition. We was gon three days and we had a hard trip to, an I had a little scourmishing with the rebs mixt with it, but they did not make mutch off of ous. We captured three prisinors

27. He is referring here to forty acres of land purchased by his dead brother Alburtus before the war.

and seven horses and we did not get a man hurt. They charged on
the rear guard of our train twice but they got as good as they sent
and I think a little better. The bullets flew around some but thay all
went too high to do any hurt. We had one horse hit and that was
all. I dont know whether any of the rebs got it slapt to any of them
or not. We ar haveing splendid wether heare and have had for
some time. It raind a little today. Thare has ben too pretty heavy
frosts heare when we was out a forageing. I stood as safeguard at a
house. They appeared to be fine folks. I eat supper with them. I
will tell you what I had warm buiscuits an pumpkin. I never saw
any such put on the table before in America but it went tip top. I
tell you, and then I had molases to put on my buiscuit. That was
the first time that I have sit down to a table in a house for over a
year. I tell you what it seemd like old times. The most of the
Regiment has draw thare pay. I have not drawn mine yet. Those
of ous that was out on the forageing expedition have not got
ourn yet, but I expect we will get it tomorrow. I will send Pa as
much as $130 dollars anyhow. Pa will get the money of Ed Maples.
The way that comes the paymaster gives the hole co. a check and
sends it to the man that the co. agreas uppon to send it to and he
dras [*sic*] [draws] the money on the check and pais it over to the
ones that we want it to go to. In doing that way thare is know danger of looseing it on the road. If the check should be captured we
would not loose it. We had an election in the Regiment today and
Father Abe got 286, and Mack [28] got thirty, so you can see how the
soldiers would go if they had a chance. Old Abe is the man to run
this show. I think as soon as the rebs find out that Abe is elected they
will pull in thare horns for they will know the war will go on four
years more and they know they cant hold out that long. So I think
they will come to some kind of terms this winter. I hope so at any
rate. I got a letter from Katie last eavening the same time I got
yours. She said that she was a going to send me a paper with it but I
did not get is. Papers ar very unsurtan about comeing through.
Friday morning. I will add a few words this morning. I have not

29. General George McClellan.

mutch time to write mutch for the mail goes out at eight o clock. I
have first got my dishes washed and the shantie swept out and I
must do some washing today. I have not had tyme to do it in the
fore part of the weak on the account of being on that forageing trip.
I dont think of anything more to write, so I will close with lots of
love to all. Your loveing Brother, Laforest.

To Mr. and Mrs. Simeon H. Dunham

Camp on Chattahoochie River, Georgia, November 4, 1864

I have not but a few minuts to write in for I am on picket. I
got the Captain to let me come in the camp a few minutes. We ar
under marching orders and we expect to start tomorrow for what
part of the globe I know not, but the talk is that we ar a going to
Savannah, Ga. If we do we will strike acrost from heare I suphose.
And if we do it ant likely that we will get a chance to write any or
get any male. I sent you $140 Dollars in a company check and you
will get the money of Ed. Maples. I have written in two or three
letters about it but I thought I had better speak about it in this, for
the other letters mite not go through. It is a cold blustering day
today. I am in hopes it will be pleasant by tomorrow if we have to
start. I got a letter from Ma and Hercey last eavening, dated on the
inside the 20th of September and on the outside the 28th. I have not
got time to write any more so I will have to close. If we dont leave
heare tomorrow I will write agaon. I will close with lots of love to
all you must not wory about me. I will do the best I can for myself,
lots of love to all. Your Loveing Son, Laforest.

To Mr. Simeon H. Dunham

Camp on Chattahoochie River, Georgia, November 5, 1864

As we did not march today, I am permitted to drop you a few
lines again. We march at seven o clock tomorrow morning. I
received your & Mas & Hercys letter of the 22nd of last month this
morning when I came in off of picket. I am well and harty and

ready for most any kind of a trip, but I dont like it mutch this time of the year. I will send you five dollars in this for I dont want but a little money with me for thare is nothing that we can buy down heare and I may be captured and that would be the last of it. I will have to stop for the mail is about ready to go out, so I close with lots of love to all, Your loveing Son Laforest.

To Miss Hercey Dunham

Camp on Chattahoochie River, Georgia, November 8, 1864

You will see by the heading of my letter that we have not left heare yet, so I will drop you a few lines to let you know how I am a getting along. I am well as usual and I hope you are well at home. I dont know whether the mail will go out today or not for day before yesterday they sed that they could not take any more, but then they thought that we would be whare they could not send it off but the mail went out yesterday so I thought I would write today and if it does you will have it ready, all though I have nothing very interesting to write. The rebs attacked our picket line yester and shot one of the 79th Ohio boys, or that is the report. The 79th Ohio is in our Brig. I hurd the fireing on the line and in a few minuts thare was a detale of 120 men out of our Regiment to strike out after the rebs and I was one of the 120. We went on quick time for about tenn miles but we could not get sight of any of them. Turned out just as I thought it would before we left camp. Just men out on foot to cach cavelry but than that is the way this show goes. Its all in a persons lifetime. We got into camp about eight o clock last eavening and we started out a litle after five. I dont know when we will leave heare now. We may stay heare all winter and then we may not be heare in an hour from now. We dont know from one hour to annother what will come next—that is the way with a soldiers life. I suppose thare is quite exsiting times in America today,[30] wouldent I like to be thar and

30. The "exciting times" referred to in this sentence were, of course, the presidential election of 1864.

vote. But after all I would not care so mutch about voting if I was only thare, but that cant be for a while yet. You wanted to know if I was letting my whiskers grow. I gues you will know me whiskers or know whiskers, but then I have not got any, but I had quite a mustch [*sic*] [mustache] but I have shaved that off now. I have not sen Chester for some time. I ment to go down to Atlanta in a day or to and see him if I can get a pass but that is prety hard to get, but I allways get one when ever I have tried. I hope Pa will get that money all right of Edward Maples. I sent five dollars more in a letter the other day. I suppose Pa had sene Major Hoskins before this time. All of the boys that ar back in the rear ar a going to go home or have gon so I suppose Lige Sclosher will go home. If Pa hase a chance to send anything to me I would like to have a pare sus- penders and a towel for we cant get any such thing down heare in this wooden country. A person might as well be on som isleland whar he would never see any one as to getting anything. I am sory that J. [Wilson] is not a comeing heare. I would like to have a good long chat with him. It would seame all most like home. Reports sais that our corps is transfurd to the arm[y] of the Tennisee and I gues it is so far. The 17 & 15 corps ar down heare now, and the army of the Cumberland, all excepting our corps, is way back some whare. I dont think of anything more to write so I will close with love to all, Your loveing Brother Laforest.

To Mr. and Mrs. Simeon H. Dunham

Camp on Chattahoochie River, Georgia, November 11, 1864

As I have a chance to send a letter right to Pontiac, I thought I would drop you a few lines to let you know that I am alive and well. We ar still heare at the River but we ar expecting to strike out evry day. The mail dont go out any more for they dont know what movement we will take of the line of march. Charlie Haney [31] is a

31. Charles Haney was a private from Pontiac Township who entered the service on September 22, 1862 and was discharged on June 8, 1865. He was also in Company C and a wartime friend of Laforest.

go in to start home on a furlow this morning. He lives down thare by the old grist mill just a crost the River. I believe our corps had quite a fight at Atlanta day before yesterday. Thare was a briggade of cavelry attacked them but they had to get up and dust in short meter. We have not hurd for sirtain what the loss was on other side. When we strike out from heare you nede not think strange if you dont heare from ous in a long time for I dont suppose that we will have a chance to send a letter untill we get to the cost [sic] [coast], the jumping place. We ar to live off of the country mostly. We had a discusen last eavening how the election went. I thought Abe would beat Mc prety bad and I tell you what we ar glad to heare of it. Have you got the money yet that I sent you in that check to Edward Maples? I hope you will get it all right. I sent you five dollars inside in a letter. I dont think of anything more to write so I will come to a close hopeing these few lines will find you all well. I close with lots of love to all. Your loveing Son, Laforest.

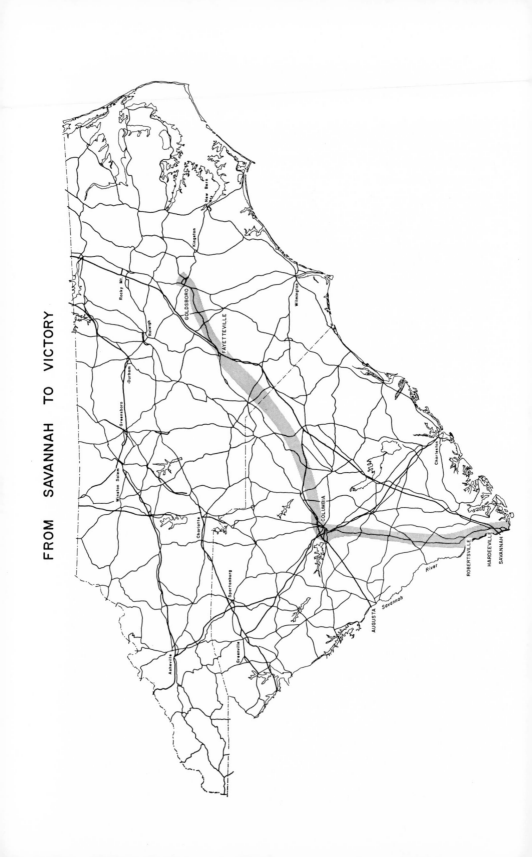

FROM SAVANNAH TO VICTORY

The Carolina Letters and the
Closing of the War
March 9, 1865–May 2, 1865

To Mr. and Mrs. Simeon H. Dunham

Goldsboro, North Carolina, March 9, 1865

I have not much news to write but I thought I would write a few lines to let you know that I am well and that we are about to start out on annother trip, whare to we do not know. We expect to start in the morning. I suppose you have heard the good news of the fall of Richmond before now. I tell you what we have had a great time heare for the last two days yelling and shouting and any amount drunk. It so the general opinion that thare wont be any more fighting. I hope thare wont but it is hard to tell. Chester was over to see me yesterday. He is as harty as ever. The report is that old Jeff is captured. I hope so but that is to good for to be true. We are having splendid wether. Four or five of our boys came up feeling bad & wer sent back sick last night, and from Atlanta the 20th Corps and the 14th Corps is called the Enemy of Georgia now. Our corps is commanded now by General Hower[1] and our Division by Gen. Ward,[2] our old Brigade commander. I have not got time to write any more now for the mail goes out at three o clock and it is about that time now. I should have commensed in time to of writen more but I supposed we would have a chance to write again in a day or two but the Ajutent come along and said the day would be our last chance. We would have [to be] on the move again. So good by for this time and lots of love to all, Laforest.

To Mr. and Mrs. Simeon H. Dunham

Goldsboro, North Carolina, March 29, 1865

After a long and teageous march we ar again whare we can heare from the loved ones at home. The first mail that we have had for two months we got day before yesterday. I have received seven letters from you since then. They wer all old letters but for all that

1. General Oliver Otis Howard who, in July of 1864, assumed the command of the Army of Tennessee.
2. Brevet Brigadier General William T. Ward.

I cant find words to express the joy that it gave me to receive them. It seams as if I could not be thankful enough that my life is spard to write to you once again. The 16th of this month we had a hard fight.[3] We wer under a heavy fire of musketry and shot and shell all day but I was fortunate enough not to get scratched. I have to stop writeing for a few minutes to have inspection of arms. I will see now if I can finish the letter without haveing to run for something. A. Ross got a letter from home stateing that Frank Johnson was dead. They must feal awful at home, three of the boys dead. Ill tell you what a person to stand it has got to be like a cast iron man. We ar haveing splendid wether heare tolerable cool nights. We have ben fixing up soom log shanties to stay in, four of ous in a shantie. We had an order read to ous from Gen. Shourman that we should now have reast and should have the best grub that they could get to ous. Capt. Calver and Hoskins got heare day before yesterday. I tell you what my boots are just the fit. I could not get a better fit if I had ben thare myself. If my life is spaird it wont be long before I will be at home, only a few days over five months before our time will be out. Whare was Joseph Wilson when he died? Just think what a change thare is since I left home. I will have to stop writeing for the mail goes out at four o clock and it is about that time now. I will write again in a day or to and I will try and write a good long one. We have know place fixt yet for writeing yet, just have to sit down on the ground and do the best that we can. Know more at present so good by for this time with lots of love to all. Laforest.

To Mr. and Mrs. Simeon H. Dunham

Goldsboro, North Carolina, March 30, 1865

I received your letter of the fifth of this month yesterday. I wrote you a few lines a day or two ago but I will try and do better

3. On March 16 the 129th met a small Confederate force at Averysboro, Taylor's Hole Creek, North Carolina. It was a short but fierce engagement won by the Union men.

this time. I tell you what I am glad to heare that you ar all well and getting along all right. I am well as usual and you know how that is. We have ben haveing splendid wether for some time untill today, it is a raining now. We have got a splendid place for a camp heare. Thare is a plenty of good spring water and then thare is a nice stream runing right along by our camp, but then thare is [no] knowing how long we will stay heare to enjoy it. We have the news heare that Richmond is taken. If that is so, and the reb army prety badly whipt, I dont think thare will be any more hard fighting to be done. We muster for pay today at tenn o clock. We have seven months due ous but I hardly think we will get paid off heare now. I will give you some thing of a discription of our trip from Savannah. When we lefe Savannah we crost the river over into S. C. and we stopt and went in to camp for tenn days at a place cald Hardieville [*sic*] [Hardeeville]. We left thare the 27th day of Jan. We marched too days and then stoped at a place called Roberts-ville. We left thare on the second of Feb. and long in the afternoon we run into the rebs and we skirmished with them untill dark. I tele you what S. C. will never forget the wipeing out that she has got. We had awful roads most of the time. We had to build co eleray [*sic*] [corduroy] roads most of the way.[4] South Carolina is prety mutch all swamp any how. I tell you what thare is not many nice houses left thare. The army took a sweap of about one hundred miles. The capital of S. C. (that is Columbia) is nothing but a forest of wals and chimneys. Our corps did not go in to the city but we wer campt on a high hill close to it so that we had a prety god view of it. It was a nice place but it has gon up now. When ever we would come to a gide board to guide a person to columbia we would put the finger pointing up (Columbia gon up). We clamd the cap-tur of Charleston and Wilmington for it was ous that drew them out of thare. We did not have any hard fighting to do untill the 16th of this month. Our brigade flanked the rebs out of a line of works. We wer right in thare rear before they new it. As soon as we got in

4. Logs were cut and split down the middle, tied together at the ends, and then laid over swampy and marshy land. It had a corduroy effect and allowed the army to move slowly through difficult terrain.

behind them we started with a yell on the doble quick and I tell you what I was never so pleased in my life as I was to see the rebs get up and try to get out of the way, but I tell you what thare was a good many of them bit the dust. I never saw the dead so thick on the field before. Prisinors that we captured said that they never saw bullets fly so thick before. They said that thare was a perfect sheat of lead going through the air. We captured four peaces of cannon and we did not have them more than five minuts before we had them turned on the rebs. On the 19th the rebs picked on to the 19 corps and drove them back, but our corps soon was in the rear of the 19 and our corps so that we did not get in to the fight. The rebs wer determined to brake our senter but they could not come it. I tell you they charged seven times on right after it. I went over and paid Chester a visit yesterday. He is well and harty. He had just got in from forageing when I got there. I dont think of anything more at present so I will close with lots of love to all, from your loveing son Laforest.

To Mr. and Mrs. Simeon H. Dunham

Washington, D.C., May 2, 1865

I thought I would drop you a few lines to let you know that I am still alive but not very harty, although nothing serious the matter. I have not received any letter from any of you for some time. I thought I would not write untill I got a letter, but I have got tiered a waiting. I expect you have stoped writeing thinking that I would be home soon. We will be ready to be mustard out today. We ar sineing the papers as fast as posible. I think we will be on our road home the first of next weak and maybe the last of this—cant start any to soon to suit me. I suppose you have seen in the papers before now about our grand review in Washington. We have a plenty to eat heare of bread, potatoes, onions, pickels. So you see that we ar liveing at the top of the pot. Chester was over heare to see me a day of two ago. I am a going over to see him this eavening. I would go today but I cant leave on the acount of signing my papers to make a sitizen out of myself, and you may bet your life that I ant any ways backward about it. I got a letter from Eugene when we first got heare. He wants me to com that way home and then he will come out home with me, but I hardly think we will go that way. The Colonel sais that we have got to go to Louisville, Ky. and thare be mustered out. I dont think of anything more to write now for if I live to get home it wont be long before we can talk in stead of writeing so good by for now with lots of love to all. Your loveing Son Laforest.

Index

DATE DUE

OCT 1 0 1970		
OCT 3 0 1970		
11/18/70		
DEC 1 1 1970		
FEB 6 1971 MT. UNION		
SEP 2 2 1976		
ORD		PRINTED IN U.S.A.